Evolution— Guilty as Charged

Frederick C. Kubicek

Treasure House

An Imprint of
Destiny Image
P.O. Box 310
Shippensburg, PA 17257

"For where your treasure is
there will your heart be also." Matthew 6:21

ISBN 1-56043-786-3

For Worldwide Distribution
Printed in the U.S.A.

Destiny Image books are available through these fine distributors outside the United States:

Christian Growth, Inc.
Jalan Kilang-Timor, Singapore 0315

Lifestream
Nottingham, England

Rhema Ministries Trading
Randburg, South Africa

Salvation Book Centre
Petaling, Jaya, Malaysia

Successful Christian Living
Capetown, Rep. of South Africa

Vision Resources
Ponsonby, Auckland, New Zealand

WA Buchanan Company
Geebung, Queensland, Australia

Word Alive
Niverville, Manitoba, Canada

Dedication

It wasn't until after I had rededicated my life to Christ in 1980 that I truly appreciated the precious gift which God had given me in the form of my family. This book is dedicated to them for all that we have been through since that eventful day.

Acknowledgment

The Most High God, who is the source of all true knowledge and the inspiration, integrity, and irrefutability of His Word.

Contents

Foreword

In the beginning God created the heaven and the earth.

Genesis 1:1, KJV

For by Him were all things created, that are in heaven, and that are in earth, visible and invisible, whether they be thrones, or dominions, or principalities, or powers: all things were created by Him, and for Him... .

Colossians 1:16, KJV

But without faith it is impossible to please Him: for he that cometh to God must believe that He is, and that He is a rewarder of them that diligently seek Him.

Hebrews 11:6, KJV

The Bible makes no attempt to prove the existence of God; it assumes it. Our great nation was founded upon Christian principles and values, and its founding fathers were creationists. They knew the plain teaching of the Scriptures: God through Jesus Christ created all things.

As a parent, I am responsible to teach this fundamental truth to my four children. As a pastor of a local church, I am responsible to teach my people the Word of God. As a Christian citizen, I am responsible to be informed.

Frederick Kubicek has done me and you a real service. Though a seasoned Bible teacher, I am a layman in the sciences. Much of what he has offered on the subject of evolution is both practical and applicable.

Evolution—Guilty as Charged is a brief, clear, and powerful presentation from a Christ-centered, Bible-based viewpoint. It will prove to be valuable reading for any concerned parent or pastor as well as classroom material for Christian schools and churches. Well-documented and to the point, this volume is an added blessing to any library.

To the author we say thanks. He has offered to us his time, expertise, and most of all, his ability to communicate information that most of us would not otherwise know.

There is hope for America and the world. We must return to the Bible and the God of the Bible. He is the Creator and we, the creation; He is the Potter and we, the clay.

Kelley Varner, Th.B., D.D.
Senior Pastor, Praise Tabernacle
Richlands, North Carolina

Introduction

The rocks which have inspired the evolutionary theory have done more to cause believers, young and old alike, to take their eyes off Jesus Christ, the Rock of our salvation, than any other single academic pursuit. This book has been written in order to bring into sharper focus the issues presented by both the theory of evolution and the biblical account of creation.

Anyone who has read any newspaper article, heard any radio program, watched any public television broadcast, or attended any university lecture which purports to deal with the topic of evolution versus creation has undoubtedly heard one or more of the following propositions set forth:

1. The evidence for the evolutionary theory of the origins of all species is both scientific and irrefutable.

2. There is no truly scientific evidence which would lead any impartial observer to conclude that the theory of special creation has any basis in fact.

3. Science is science, and religion is religion. They are like oil and water; they do not now, nor have they ever, mixed well with each other.

4. Any discussion of creationism is by definition religious in nature and should therefore not be allowed in any public school classroom.

5. The theory of evolution and the Genesis account of creation are compatible when viewed through the eyes of reason.

6. There is every reason to believe that God used the method of evolution to "create" the world and the universe.

7. There is absolutely no relationship between the scientific theory of evolution and the philosophical position which has been labeled by some fundamentalist Christians as "secular humanism."

Much of the evidence which has been put forth in support of the aforementioned positions is examined within the pages of this book. Of equal importance though is the fact that numerous items which totally disprove each of the above-mentioned positions also are presented and analyzed herein.

As this material is read and investigated, it will become clear that many proponents of the theory of evolution are totally ignorant of the vast number of scientific and historic facts which totally disprove their theory. It will also become obvious rather quickly that a substantial number of evolution's most vocal advocates have been guilty of intentionally withholding from the public the very evidence which disproves Darwin's theory. In addition, evidence will be presented which proves that evolutionists have used fraudulent exhibits, eloquently fabricated stories, circular reasoning, and misleading statements in their unending attempts to remove all vestiges of Christianity not only from our public school classrooms, but from the very minds of America's children.

Chapter 1

More Than Genesis

"In the beginning God created the heavens and the earth" (Gen. 1:1). What a simple, beautiful, and concise statement that is. I firmly believe that all people who call themselves Christians accept that opening verse of God's Word as being literally true. The difficulty seems to arise among some believers when they get to verse 2 and go on through chapter 2 verse 26.

Every article I have written to this point in time has been based upon my understanding that the Bible is the divinely inspired Word of God (see Acts 4:25; Jer. 1:12; 2 Pet. 1:21; 1 Thess. 2:13; Ps. 18:30; Ps. 12:6; 2 Tim. 3:16; Ex. 9:35; Prov. 30:5; Ps. 119:89,152,160; 1 Pet. 1:25; Is. 40:8; Ps. 33:4; Ps. 111:7; Rom. 15:4; Prov. 30:6). These articles also have been based upon a literal interpretation of biblical words and phrases within the context in which they appear. This book has been written upon the foundation of these same two assumptions. By no means is it intended to be an all-encompassing treatment of the subject of creation versus evolution. However, it is intended to address some of the major issues of this topic as they are presented by both the Bible and that which many people maintain is the "scientific" theory of evolution.

Some Christians, in an attempt to reconcile the scriptural account of creation with what they perceive to be irrefutable proof for the theory of evolution, discount the first two chapters of Genesis as mere poetry. If in fact these chapters were poetic in nature, then it would not be necessary to apply the literal meaning to the word *day* found therein. The problem with the poetic view of Genesis chapters 1 and 2 is that the repetition, parallelism, and meter found in *all* scriptural poetry is conspicuously absent. More important, any attempt to correlate the two divergent concepts of the origin of man presented by the theory of evolution and Genesis 1 and 2 requires that some very specific statements of Jesus Christ also be dismissed as either poetic or fictional.

Jesus not only refers to the fact that God created the world, but He specifically states that man was created at the beginning of creation (see Mk. 10:6; see also Mt. 19:4). This verse does not require us to believe that man was created on the first day, rather that he was created within the confines of the seven-day week of creation and not 4 billion years after the process began. We notice a similar vein in Romans 1:20 (NEB), which clearly implies that someone has been around from the beginning to perceive God's handiwork when it says, "…His everlasting power and Deity have been visible ever since the world began." In order to bring the biblical account of creation into line with evolution, it would be necessary to rewrite this verse to read, "…His everlasting power and Deity were not visible until about 4 billion years after the world began."

In First Corinthians 15:45 Paul gives further credence to a literal interpretation of Genesis 1 and 2 because he accepts as reality the fact that the first man was named Adam and not Olduvai George-*Homo erectus*. (The latter is a rather satirical name given to one of the fossil discoveries of the Leakey family which was reported in *Newsweek*, February 13, 1967.) Paul reaffirms his faith in the Genesis account of creation by stating that all the nations on earth came from Adam (through Noah) and not from the simultaneous development of the same species at several different locations throughout the world (see Acts 17:26). He further states the fact that females did not evolve along with males, but were created by God as described in Genesis 2:21-22 (see 1 Cor. 11:9).

Do not be confused by those who claim that Genesis chapters 1 and 2 actually contain two separate conflicting accounts of creation. Many people choose to see a conflict where none in fact exists. Genesis 1:1-2:2 provides us with one narration of the events which occurred during the seven-day week of creation. Genesis 2:4-24 contains a separate account of the same period. By no means are these reports conflicting. As is so often the case, any perceived conflict is only in the eye of the beholder.

That one statement highlights or expands upon some portion of an event does not mean that it conflicts with another description which emphasizes other areas. Genesis 1 and 2 do not contain conflicting accounts of creation, but complementary ones. You need not rely upon my word alone concerning this. In Matthew 19:4 Jesus specifically referred to Genesis 1:27 when He stated that God created "male and female." He then referred to Genesis 2:24 as He continued His thoughts in Matthew 19:5-6, telling us that husbands and wives are "one flesh." Needless to say, in that Jesus quoted from *both chapters* during His discussion of the *single* act of creation, it can easily be seen that He saw no conflict.

The point however is still the same. More than just Genesis 1 and 2 must be dismissed if evolution is to be accepted, because the Genesis account of creation is referred to as fact throughout the Bible. Moses specifically restates it in Exodus 31:17, as does Isaiah in Isaiah 45:12,18, Nehemiah in Nehemiah 9:6, Jeremiah in Jeremiah 27:5, Solomon in Proverbs 8:29, Zechariah in Zechariah 12:1, and David in Psalm 148:3-5. Genesis 1:16 informs us that God "made the stars," and Amos 5:8 and Job 38:32 and 9:9 even list some of the specific constellations. Genesis 1:10 tells us that God gathered the waters together and called them seas, and so do Psalm 95:5 and 78:13 and Revelation 10:6. Genesis 1:24-25 says that the animals, both wild and domestic, were created by God, and Jeremiah 27:5 reaffirms this. As we saw earlier, Jesus left no room for doubt when He said that God created man, but then neither do Genesis 5:1-5 and 6:7 and Deuteronomy 4:32.

Not only do we have those specific verses which say that God did the creating, but we can turn to Colossians 1:17, Hebrews 1:3, and Jeremiah 33:25 and find that it is His power which sustains the universe and assures us of its continuing existence. (See also Ps. 148:6.) There are numerous other verses which speak of God's creation. As examples see 2 Kings 19:15; 1 Chronicles 16:26; Psalm 96:5; 115:15; 121:2; 124:8; 134:3; 146:6; Proverbs 8:26; Psalm 24:1; 119:90; 136:6; 104:5; Job 38:31; Isaiah 51:13,16; John 1:3; Acts 14:15; 17:24; Mark 13:19; Isaiah 48:13, Colossians 1:16; Revelation 4:11; Amos 4:13; Isaiah 40:28; Psalm

89:11-12; 148:5; Jeremiah 27:5; Isaiah 17:7; Proverbs 20:12; Psalm 94:9; 136:7-9; 33:6. Throughout Scripture God reminds us that He did the creating and that He did it exactly as He said He did.

Does that then mean that of necessity a literal 24-hour day is referred to in Genesis 1:5,8,13,19,23 and 31? I believe that is exactly what the Scriptures do show us. These six verses clearly state that with each day there was an evening and a morning. The Hebrew word for morning used therein is *boker*, which means "dawn, as the break of day" (*Strong's Concordance* no. 1242). According to *Wigram's Hebrew Concordance*, which lists every verse in which the Hebrew word is used in the original Hebrew text regardless of how it may have been translated into English, the word *boker* is used 182 other times in the Old Testament. Every time it is used it is referring to those hours in the early part of the day which we customarily think of as *morning*. How could I now say that the word boker means a literal morning 182 times, but something else the six times it is used in Genesis chapter 1?

The Hebrew word for evening used in the above six verses of Genesis chapter 1 is *erev*, meaning "dusk, eventide" (*Strong's Concordance* no. 6153). The other 124 times it is used throughout the Old Testament it refers to those hours at the end of a 24-hour day which we usually associate with *evening*. Again, how could I now give a meaning to the word *erev* in Genesis 1 other than the literal *evening* it implies the other 124 times it is used? If each day was in fact a thousand years and had a morning and evening, then each of those times would have been about 500 years long. Needless to say, it would have gotten very, very hot in the "morning" and very, very cold in the "evening." These are not exactly ideal growing conditions for plants which require photosynthesis to survive.

This does not put us in conflict with Second Peter 3:8, which says, "With the Lord a day is like a thousand years, and a thousand years are like a day." In the context, we see that Peter was discussing a topic for which God had given no exact time reference, namely, the coming judgment of mankind. Then as now critics were saying, "Where is this 'coming' He promised? Ever since our fathers died, everything goes on as it has since the beginning of creation" (1 Pet. 3:4). Peter was answering those skeptics by saying in effect, "Don't make the mistake of thinking that just because it hasn't happened yet, it won't happen." To assume that Peter's statement in verse 8 deals with the fleeting reference to creation made by those skeptics is to violate every concept of both literary criticism and biblical interpretation. It would make as much sense to say that the Feast of Tabernacles mentioned in Leviticus 23:34 was to last 7 thousand years simply because it was to last for "seven days."

God *has* given us a specific time frame concerning creation, and it is found in the word *day* which is the correct interpretation of the Hebrew word *yom* (no. 3117 in *Wigram's Concordance* and listed as yom, no. 3117 in *Strong's Concordance*). In Genesis 1:5,8,13,19,23 and 31 it is used in direct conjunction with an ordinal to indicate a specific day. An example of this is verse 5, "And there was evening, and there was morning—the first day." Throughout the Old Testament the word *yom* is used 350 additional times in direct conjunction with an ordinal or a numeral. Every single time it is so used, it refers to a literal 24-hour period of time. Where is the justification for now saying that it means something other than that in Genesis 1:5,8,13,19,23 and 31?

Since we know that God usually speaks to us twice concerning major theological issues (Job 33:14 and Gen. 41:32) we should expect to find a second reference to creation within the framework of a literal 24-hour period, if in fact that is what God intends for us to believe. Exodus 20:8-11 tells us that God established the Sabbath day for Israel because, "For in six days the Lord made the heavens and the earth, the sea, and all that is in them, but He rested on the seventh..." (see also Ex. 31:17). Here God is speaking to Moses (Ex. 20:1) and He is making a direct correlation between man's six literal days (*yom*) of work and His six literal days (*yom*) of creation. He is directing man to rest one day (*yom*) just as He rested one day (*yom*). Furthermore, we are shown in Exodus 31:18 that God not only spoke these words to Moses, but wrote them Himself on the stone tablets. One additional point to consider while on this topic is that it cannot be said that God's rest on the seventh day lasted a thousand years or, as some would have us believe, is still going on, because as we have already seen in Colossians 1:17 and Hebrews 1:3 God is still sustaining the world and holding it together by His power.

There is yet another theological concept which deals with the issue of time and which needs to be mentioned here. This is known as the gap theory or the restoration theory. According to the gap theory, Genesis 1:1 is indeed correct. So is Genesis 1:2. However, its adherents believe that between 4.5 and 5 billion years separate the time frame of the two verses.

Adherents to this position assume that the dinosaurs roamed the earth during this gap period. At some point an overwhelming cataclysm occurred, which may very well have been the result of the rebellion referred to in Ezekiel 28.

As a result of this event God's first creation became desolate. They interpret Genesis 1:2 to read, "Now the earth *became* formless and empty...," instead of, "Now the earth *was* formless and empty...." In other words, they would have us believe that Genesis 1:2 through 2:3 is actually the account of God's *second* creation or *re*creation of the earth, with the first creation having occurred almost 5 billion years earlier. To them, the fossils which are found today, both animal and human, are actually the remains of God's *first* creation.

There are numerous conservative theologians who reject the theory of evolution, but who hold to this position for other reasons. However, there are many other theologians who rely on the gap theory for no reason other than they are under the misguided impression that the evidence which supports the theory of evolution is so overwhelming that it must be true. In effect, they have attempted to reconcile their belief in the Genesis account of creation with the evidence for evolution by relying upon the gap theory.

This may sound logical, but like the theory of evolution itself, the gap theory requires those who believe it to ignore numerous other verses of the Bible. It also gives meanings to words which are contrary to those found throughout the rest of Scripture. For example, those who hold to the gap theory would translate the Hebrew word *hayah* in Genesis 1:2 as *became*. Now, this word is used 1,500 times in the first five books of the Old Testament alone to denote the word was. The Hebrew word normally translated *became* is *haphak*, and that word is not found in Genesis 1:2. Furthermore, the use of the Hebrew connective *vav* at the beginning of Genesis 1:2 emphasizes that the condition referred to therein follows immediately on the heels of the creating action mentioned in verse 1. (Note also that the New English Bible, the Jerusalem Bible, and New American Standard, Moffat, and every other modern translation of the Bible correctly use the word *was* in Genesis 1:2, not the word *became* upon which gap theory advocates insist.)

Further proof that no gap exists between Genesis 1:1 and 1:2 is found in Genesis 2:1-3 and Exodus 20:11. Therein we are told that God created the "*heavens* and the earth" in six days. Since the only place that the word *heavens* can be found in Genesis chapter 1 is in verse 1, it must be assumed that the heavens and earth of verse 1 were part of the six-day creation process referred to in the remainder of the chapter, not the product of some previous creation which occurred 5 billion years earlier.

Another point to consider is this: Evolutionists maintain that the fossil record proves that tens of thousands of species of animals existed before the first humans evolved, and most of these creatures died off before man appeared. If such is the case, death existed long before Adam sinned. This of course puts the gap theory in direct conflict with Romans 5:12, which indicates that death entered the world only after Adam sinned. If the fossils we find today are in fact the remains of *dead animals* which lived on some previous earth, how could God have said that the earth He recreated in Genesis 1:9 was "very good"? Besides, when you consider the fact that evolution relies upon death and extinction in order to work and produces a tremendous number of "dead ends" in the process, it is illogical to assume that the God of the entire universe would use such an inefficient mechanism as evolution for His creating process (1 Cor. 14:33). Finally, how could God have said in Hebrews 11:3 (NEB), "…that the visible came forth from the invisible," if the earth we see today were made from already existing elements (fossils)? Obviously those fossils and the cataclysm which led to their formation must have occurred at some point *after* God's "very good" creation.

Keep in mind that there is no scriptural evidence to support the claim that there was any *earthly* catastrophic consequence related to the events of Ezekiel 28 or Isaiah 14 as they are traditionally interpreted. It is also equally incorrect to argue that there was some heavenly cataclysm associated with these events. Since only the earth is mentioned in verse 2 of Genesis chapter 1, there is no scriptural evidence to even suggest, let alone prove, that the heavens *became* void. Therefore, according to the gap theory, these heavens must have existed during the 5 billion year gap without a sun, a moon, or stars, because these heavenly bodies were not created for the first time until the fourth day of the six-day creation week.

We need to be aware that those who attempt to correlate the biblical account of creation with the theory of evolution run into still another problem. Evolutionists will tell you that the solar system was the first entity to come into existence, whereas Genesis 1:14-19 informs us that this did not occur until the fourth day of creation. Evolutionists will tell you that the planets (including earth) were flung out from the sun—which is a star—after the solar system appeared. On the other hand, Genesis tells us that the earth came before any of the stars. Evolutionists will tell you that marine invertebrates and even fish evolved before land plants appeared.

However Genesis 1:9-12 reveals the fact that *all* land vegetation preceded the creation of marine life. Finally, the evolutionists will say that animals, amphibians, and sharks all were established prior to the appearance of the forests, but Genesis 1:20-25 indicates that these were in fact created after the forests.

There is however an even greater obstacle which must be overcome by any believer who desires to correlate Genesis with Darwin's theory by saying that God used the method of evolution to accomplish the act of creation. That problem is the presupposition which evolutionists such as Niles Eldredge, a curator with the American Museum of Natural History, maintain is the cornerstone of their theory. To Eldredge evolution is science, and science requires that the notion of a creator be set aside.[1] At a recent gathering of the National Science Teachers' Association in Kansas City, Carl Sagan expressed his disdain for the perfectly valid, nonevolutionary academic pursuit known as scientific creationism by referring to it as nothing more than an "oxymoronic subject."[2]

By no means though are Eldredge and Sagan the only evolutionists who make this assumption. Those of us who watch TV have undoubtedly heard similar sentiments expressed on the public broadcasting system. For example, William B. Provine said,

> The vast majority of people believe there is a design
> …in the universe [and] that it is somehow responsible
> for both the visible and moral order of the world.
> Modern biology has undermined this assumption.
> Even though it is often asserted that science is fully

compatible with our Judeo/Christian ethical tradition, in fact it is not... ..[3]

Perhaps also those of us who read magazines such as *National Geographic* have seen assertions such as the following from the pen of no less than its editor, Wilbur Garrett:

There are as many different myths, such as the Judeo/Christian story of God creating first a man and then a woman in the Garden of Eden, as there are ancient cultures. Scientists dismiss the myths... .[4]

Needless to say, it would appear that at least as far as the evolutionists are concerned, there is no way that the Genesis account of creation can be made to square with their brand of science. Isaac Asimov acknowledged that "Any real comparison between what the Bible says and what the [evolutionistic] astronomer thinks shows us instantly that the two have virtually nothing in common."[5] To put it bluntly, if the concept of evolution as it applies to the origin of the species is correct, then the Bible is wrong.

It has been said that Jesus Christ is one of three things: either He is a liar, a lunatic, or He is who He says He is. (I believe that He is who He says He is.) the same type of thing can be said regarding creation; either God created the world as He says He did or He didn't, in which case He would be a liar, and God is not a man that He should lie (Tit. 1:2; Heb. 6:18, 1 Sam. 15:29; 2 Sam. 7:28; Num. 23:19; Is. 45:19).

Chapter 2

I'd Rather Not Talk About It

My quarrel is not with true science, but with a theory (which in reality is little more than an hypothesis) that is passed off as scientific, when in fact it cannot even meet the first and foremost test of what it is that makes an idea scientific. Eldredge states in part that for an idea to be scientific, it must be an explanation of some phenomenon which is "testable solely by the criteria of our five senses."[1] I do not disagree with this statement. However, by its very nature the theory of evolution is totally unscientific because it is impossible to test any hypothesis which by its own definition requires 4 billion years to work. Yet, evolutionists maintain that evolution is as scientific as the study of quantum mechanics.[2]

A prime example of such incongruous logic is furnished by Eldredge himself. In his book, *The Monkey Business: A Scientist Looks at Creationism*, he passes along the hypothesis that the development of oxygen in the atmosphere at a level high enough to support complex life came about as the by-product of photosynthesis in algae over a period of several "billions" of years. He then states that "such an hypothesis is difficult to test," but he appears to accept it himself because he offers no alternative to it and merely continues on with his discussion.[3]

Eldredge appears to accept as part of his "science" an idea which is not only *difficult* to test, but is downright *impossible* to test by the criteria of our five senses. But then Eldredge is certainly not alone in his inability to provide truly scientific explanations to such foundational questions. The best that Rick Gore, assistant editor of *National Geographic*, could do was say that "…certain bacterial members of the primordial slime *invented* the kind of photosynthesis that releases oxygen as a waste produce."[4] The acceptance or willingness to accept as "scientific" an idea which violates the very rule of what it is that makes an idea scientific must raise some question in the reader's mind as to exactly how "scientific" evolution really is.

The simple fact that evolutionists call their study scientific does not make it so, even if they have been doing it for a hundred years and insist that it be treated as such in our children's textbooks. The fact that Eldredge states that "all reputable biological scientists see evolution as the only naturalistic scientific explanation of the order we see in the biological side of nature" should not defame the character of any biologist who accepts the Genesis account of creation, although the inference is clearly made.[5]

What then can we expect the pseudoscience of evolution to tell us? Dr. Stephen Jay Gould of Harvard University provided us with part of the answer to that question in a speech he gave before a group of evolutionists at Hobart

College, wherein he stated that "...if it doesn't agree with your idea you don't talk about it."[6] (By the way, Dr. Gould is not a creationist. In fact, he is coauthor with Niles Eldredge of the currently popular "punctuated equilibria" theory which is used by evolutionists to explain why it is that the fossil record in reality does *not* show gradual evolution.) Now, while there are other things we can expect from evolutionsts, let us first take a look at the points which do not appear in school textbooks and which definitely do not support the theory of evolution.

The fossil record is at the very heart of the theory of evolution, and it is there that I would like to begin this part of our study. Darwin believed that the different species developed one from another, either by direct descent or through a common ancestor and that complex life forms developed gradually over millions of years from simpler forms. This basic definition of evolution is still found in student texts such as *Webster's New World Dictionary With Student Handbook*, 1978 edition, which says that evolution is "the gradual changes that take place as something develops into its *final form*." However, Darwin himself noted, "Geology assuredly does not reveal such finely graduated organic chains...the explanation lies, I believe, in the extreme imperfection of the geological record."[7] That record is no longer "imperfect" in that there are currently more than 100 million categorized fossils in the world's museums, and no graduated chain can be found.[8]

Evolutionists regularly accuse those who believe in the Genesis account of creation of attacking the *science* of geology and the *science* of paleontology whenever they point out all the inconsistencies of the evolutionists' position. That is a good smoke screen because it immediately puts the Christian on the defensive. This is unfortunate because it is not the science of geology or the science of paleontology which is under fire. After all, geology and paleontology are legitimate sciences, and I know of no one who wishes to attack the study of the earth or fossils when such studies follow established scientific principles. What is under attack is the type of sloppy, closed-minded scholarship exhibited by some geologists and paleontologists who are confirmed evolutionists and who, using Edlredge's own words, "Spoke eloquently of the ravages of time, the erosion and metamorphism that destroyed the older vestiges of the fossil record," when in fact there was no evidence to suggest that any "older vestiges" every existed in the first place.[9] Even Eldredge is forced to admit that many of his past colleagues were "...adventurous thinkers...[who used their] active imagination [to] *invent* novel explanations of how evolution takes place."[10]

These men made every effort to explain something which never existed, that is, the evidence of the gradual evolution of the species which Darwin assumed was there. Their preconceived notion that the fossil record had to eventually yield something they "knew" was there caused them to assure our parents, and us, and if you will check your child's science book you will most likely find that they still are assuring our children, that it is a "scientific fact" that we *slowly* evolved from single-celled life forms. In fact, that is not what the fossil record shows at all. Such assertions were not scientific when they were made. In reality, they were nothing more than wishful thinking on the part of those who made them.

Every single major invertebrate form of life is found in the rock strata known as Cambrian, and yet not a single, indisputable, multicellular fossil has ever been found in Precambrian rock. The sudden appearance of all those life forms in Cambrian rock is even acknowledged by Eldredge to be "perhaps the greatest of all events in life's history," yet its explanation is, according to him, *"a mystery."*[11] The very foundation of organic evolution is categorized as a mystery because *no* evidence exists to fit the evolutionists' preconceived theory of evolution.

To me, however, the astounding thing is that evolutionists refer to the sudden appearance of every major invertebrate form of life as "evolutionary" when not one shred of fossil evidence exists to suggest (let alone prove) that there had been any type of gradual development from the less complex to the more complex multicellular forms of life which are indisputably present in the Cambrian rock formation. In an attempt to explain the lack of Precambrian multicellular fossils Eldredge says, "…the intermediates had to have been soft bodied, and thus extremely unlikely to become fossilized."[12] That sounds logical, and were it not for some other seldom discussed points, many of us would believe it.

But that explanation ignores the fact that fossils of worms and caterpillars have been found by L.S.B. Leakey in other strata.[13] Hair, feathers, and stomach contents along with other soft body tissues have been found in the fossil beds of central Germany.[14] Just as interesting though is the fact that such an explanation ignores the fossils of seven-foot-long jellyfish, worms, and sponges found in the Cambrian rock itself— and you can't get much more softbodied than that. The most

most intriguing thing of all is that fossils of flowering plants and fish also have been found in Cambrian rock, and they weren't supposed to have been evolved at the time that Cambrian rock was being formed.[15]

At this point in our study, however, the most important thing to remember is that there is no evidence in any rock strata of the gradualness Darwin's theory demanded, and this fact is not contained in our children's high school textbooks.

Student textbooks still contain statements such as this one by William H. Matthews III, "Fossils provide one of the strongest lines of evidence to support the theory of organic evolution."[16] Note also this one by Twenhofel and Shreik, "No line of evidence more forcefully and clearly supports the fundamental principle of evolution—descent with accumulative modification—than that furnished by the fossils."[17] Even more detailed reference books (such as major encyclopedias) tell us that fossils present "evidence to support the theory of evolution," which is itself defined as a "process of gradual change," that explains how "organisms gradually developed specialized characteristics that helped them adapt to their environment."[18] All of these statements, remember, are made in spite of the fact that at the very first level in which multicellular fossils are found (Cambrian rock) there is absolutely *no* evidence of "accumulative modification." It is also clear from other observations that while "transitions" at the subspecies level are observable, they are only inferable at the species level and *totally absent between higher categories.*[19]

This absence of higher life form transitions was first mentioned by Professor Richard Goldschmidt of the University of California at Berkeley in 1940. He specifically noted that "transitions between higher categories are missing."[20] In fact, this lack of transitions is so obvious that Professor George Gaylord Simpson, a vertebrate paleontologist at Harvard University, stated that "higher transitions are not recorded because they did not exist... ."[21] Dr. Austin Clark, a biologist with the Smithsonian Institution, stated that "since we have not the slightest evidence among the living or fossil animals of any integrating types following between major groups it is a fair supposition that there never have been, any such integrating types."[22] It would seem that this complete absence of transition fossils has been noted everywhere except in our children's textbooks.

Dr. Stephen Jay Gould states that the "fossil record offered no support for gradual change...new species *almost always appeared suddenly* in the fossil record with no intermediate links to ancestors in the older rock of the same region."[23] Along the same line Eldredge makes an interesting observation concerning life-cycle changes which the fossil record does show. "Such changes have *not been graceful.* Life has been occasionally violently disrupted by major episodes of extinction that appear to have eliminated 75% or more of *all* species in some cases."[24]

The preceding five quotes were not taken from creationists, but from confirmed evolutionists. Their words tell us that the 125 years of *graduated* evolutionary teaching that had been and still is being taught as "scientific fact," simply is not true. In fact, Dr. Colin Patterson, senior paleontologist at the British Museum of Natural History, has gone so far as to state that "statements about ancestry [of species] are not applicable in the fossil record... [but] are *made up stories...not part of science.*"[25]

Before we proceed any further I would like to highlight what has just been said because the consequences of these rather surprising admissions by members of the evolutionary community are indeed astounding. I am sure that we all have heard the expression *evolutionary chain* or *missing link*. In using the term *missing link* I am not referring to its more limited definitions, i.e., as it applies only to man's supposed ancestors, but to its more general meaning as it applies to the development of every species within the animal kingdom. I am, however, going to limit this part of our discussion to the "higher categories" of scientific classification known as families, as opposed to the final level of classification known as species.

Imagine for a moment that one representative from each extinct and living family of animals is standing before you holding a link of steel chain in its hand (or paw or foot, whichever you prefer). Each one of these 10 thousand or so specimens would then take its assigned place in the so-called evolutionary chain of development and begin looking around for that "ancestor" with whom it could join its link. No doubt what you would notice is that all 10 thousand specimens were standing there with a blank expression on their faces. This of course results from the fact that not one of them could find anyone, either from among the living or the extinct, which directly preceded them in this supposed chain. There is no one with whom they could link up. You see, there is not merely one missing link, but 10 thousand of them, and that is at the family level alone. If we go down to the species level of classification, the number of missing links increases by the tens of thousands because as we have just seen, even the evolutionists now admit that there is absolutely no evidence in the fossil record of graduated transitional forms.

The question now is will the evolutionists graciously accept the account of creation as set forth in Genesis? They cannot! Remember, Eldredge stated at the outset that a purely evolutionistic scientist must of necessity deny the existence of a Creator God. The evolutionists absolute prejudice against a creator is best summed up in the words of D.M.S. Watson, a frequent commentator on the BBC and himself an evolutionist. He stated that "evolution itself is accepted by zoologists not because it has been observed to occur, or can be proven logically by coherent evidence to be true, but because the only alternative, special creation, is clearly incredible."[26] Such an attitude therefore causes the evolutionists to totally dismiss even the evidence of the very fossils they must of necessity depend upon, when those fossils do not line up with their preconceived notions that life gradually appeared over millions of years.

Referring to the catastrophic changes mentioned earlier, Eldredge states, "…such events…took upwards of a million years to accomplish. But once again, such long periods show up as dramatically sudden turnovers if the rock record is taken literally."[27] How incredible! For decades we were told that the fossil record is at the very heart of evolutionary evidence. Now we are told that we shouldn't take it literally in this case because such a literal interpretation does not fit the preconceived notion of time which we were assured the rock record supported. In one breath Eldredge chides his past colleagues because they didn't take the fossil record literally and accept what any literal interpretation of Genesis chapters 1 and 2 would have told them, i.e., that there were no gradual changes; in the next breath he tells us not to take the rock record literally because if we do, we won't end up with as many millions of years as the evolutionist needs in order for his theory to have even the slightest chance of working out.

Why would Eldredge say such things? Simply because his theory of punctuated equilibria uses a literal interpretation of the fossil record to show no gradual changes, but like any other evolutionist, he still needs millions of years to increase the statistical possibilities that other portions of his theory will work out. He must therefore deny the literal interpretation of the rock record when such an interpretation would knock several million years off his time clock.

Since the rock record does not show the gradual changes formerly insisted upon by evolutionists, the inevitable has finally happened. As Eldredge and Gould now maintain, "...the fossil record...suggests to some of us that some of the specific ideas that Darwin and many of his successors right up to the present day, had on how life evolves, may be at least partially wrong."[28] They have as inconspicuously as possible thrown out the first major tenet of Darwin's theory, i.e., the gradual evolution of every species over long periods of time. They and an apparent majority of the nation's leading biological evolutionists who attended a conference in October 1980 at the Field Museum of Natural History in Chicago now accept what is known as punctuated equilibria.

Translated into common English, this means that the species are, were, and will most likely remain separated from each other by a division of some type.[29] In short, there are no gradual changes from one species to another. While there may be gradual changes *within* species, for example, men of the 20th century are taller than men of the 15th century, there had to be sudden, numerous, major organic changes within a short span of time in order to explain the sudden appearance of different species. They say it happened over thousands of years (as opposed to the previously alleged "fact" that it took millions of years), but as far as the fossil record is concerned, it could just as easily have happened over the span of one generation—but they will not admit that.

However, as was the case with Darwin's gradualism, there is absolutely no fossil evidence to prove the punctuated equilibria hypothesis, as there are still no fossilized transitions. In an attempt to explain this problem, evolutionists who hold to this notion maintain that these changes affected relatively few animals. In short, greater chances affecting fewer animals over a shorter period of time meant that fewer specimens were available to even have a chance to become fossilized. In any case, the sudden changes that they now assure us happened fly directly in the face of Charles Darwin's own statement, "...if it could be demonstrated that any complex organ exists which could not possibly have been formed by numerous successive slight modifications, *my theory would absolutely break down.*"[30]

Eldredge and Gould are on the leading edge of the currently popular evolutionary thought which maintains that sudden changes are exactly what happened, but they still refuse to accept what Darwin himself said would be the only possible consequence of such a finding, namely, "...my theory would absolutely break down." If that isn't bad enough, look at what they offer as a "scientific" replacement for Darwin's gradualism—punctuated equilibria, an hypothesis which even they admit "*isn't* particularly neat, elegant, all-embracing, *completely testable*, or even as yet *totally thought through*."[31] Nevertheless, we are supposed to accept this nontestable idea as scientific, even though it violates the very rule which Eldredge himself said must be met before an idea can be considered scientific.

This is not the end of the problems which the fossil record presents to the evolutionist. Among other problems are fossilized trees—some right side up and some upside down—penetrating several different strata of rock. Obviously, this is something which could not have happened unless both the tree and the different strata were laid down at the same time.[32] There are also numerous areas, such as the Cumberland Bone Cave in Maryland, where fossils of mammals, birds, and reptiles from different types of climates have been found mixed together, and there are fossil beds so huge that nothing short of some worldwide cataclysm could possibly explain them. Examples of these huge beds are the Karoo formation in South Africa, containing an estimated 800 billion vertebrate skeletons, and the hippopotamus beds of Sicily which are extensive enough that they have been mined commercially for charcoal. The thousands of frozen mammoths found in Siberia should also be included in this group.

The final problem which I will mention that the fossil record presents deals with where the fossils themselves are located. According to traditional evolutionistic thoughts, the oldest fossils are the least complex and should be found in the lowest rock strata while the newer, more complex fossils would appear only in the upper strata. (While this is generally found to be true, evolutionists ignore the fact that this could just as well be explained by the biblical great flood. In such a situation the more able-bodied, complex life forms would have sought higher ground and would be the last to die and therefore the last to have become buried under the sediment produced by the flood. Note also that the sediment itself would have been deposited in layers as the flood waters receded from the earth.) What are normally not discussed in high school textbooks are the glaring exceptions to the evolutionists' traditional position.

In fact, these exceptions are so numerous that some geologists who are themselves strongly committed to the evolutionists' overall viewpoint now admit that the "simple to complex" premise held by many of their colleagues simply is not supported by the fossil record. They point out that while it is indeed true that the fossil remains of simple organisms are found in lower rock strata and the fossil remains of complex animals are found in higher strata, this fact alone does not establish an evolutionary chain. David M. Raup of the University of Chicago correctly notes that within the fossil record "there is *no recognizable trend toward increased complexity* that is clear enough to use for dating purposes.... . Even where the fossil record of a coherent group of organisms can be traced...*increasing complexity through time is elusive at best.* "[33] Besides, to compare the complexity of an insect with the simplicity of a starfish is to compare apples to oranges.

Concerning the location of simple fossils vis-à-vis more complex ones, it should also be noted that in the mountainous regions of every continent numerous examples can be found where the less complex fossils are on top of the more complex ones.[34] Geologists have a name for formations such as these where fossils appear to be out of sequence, they call them "overthrusts." In an overthrust the bottom layer of rock is said to have slid over on top of the neighboring newer strata. Evolutionists will tell you that this is exactly what happened with the Lewis overthrusts in Montana, that is assuming that they mention it at all.

Even if they do mention the Lewis overthrust, what they probably will not point out to you is that it is over 6 miles wide in places and ranges in length from 135 to 350 miles. Now that is one huge piece of rock to move by slow natural means, but that is what they want us to believe. What's more is that they want us to believe that it moved more than 30 miles to its present location and did so without leaving sufficient signs to demonstrate such a massive shift of the earth's surface. While it is true that the area may indeed be described as geologically disturbed, the disturbances noted cannot account for a relocation of this magnitude. Evolutionists would also ask us to believe that the Matterhorn mountain in the Swiss Alps moved at least 20 miles to its present location and that Mythen Peak, which has what is estimated to be 200-million-year-old rock on top of 60-million-year-old rock, moved from Africa to Switzerland.[35]

This brings us to another example of the incongruous thinking which is used by the evolutionist. One of the reasons some evolutionists reject any concept of a creator is that such a concept brings into play a god who, according to their reasoning, must have acted "using laws no longer in operation," and such a possibility is "utterly beyond the purview of science."[36] If we assume that this statement represents the overall point of view held by members of the evolutionistic community, it reveals three interesting things about their mind-set. First, evolutionists have made a "god" of their "science" in that they have defined the limits within which anything can, has, or will operate.[37] Secondly, they believe that God does not act today as He did at the creation. This belief causes them to not only deny the first two chapters of Genesis, but the crossing of the Red Sea as described in Exodus 14:21-22, Jesus' walking on the water as related in Matthew 14:25, and any number of totally miraculous healings which have happened in the past few years alone, including the creation of new eyeballs in previously empty sockets. Thirdly, and most importantly for purposes of this discussion, evolutionists place total confidence in a concept known as uniformitarianism. This concept assumes that the forces of nature acting today are sufficient to account for all past geological changes.

Charles Lyell, the father of modern evolutionistic geology, developed this concept by expanding upon the ideas of his predecessor, James Hutton. He was strongly opposed to any explanation of a geological event which even suggested catastrophe. To quote Lyell, "...no causes whatever have from the earliest time...to the present, ever acted, but those now acting; and *they have never acted with different degrees of energy from that which they now exert.*"[38] Traditionally, evolutionists have taken the position that Lyell "dealt catastrophism the death blow."[39] Therefore, if any evolutionist tells you that he now accepts certain types of catastrophic changes, he is again eliminating one of the major suppositions that made up the foundations of his theory. Not only that, but in the process he has actually created a major intellectual dilemma for himself.

Eldredge points out that the geologic column (which evolutionists used to establish the earth's age) was worked out before Darwin published his *Origin of the Species*. This of course is quite true. However, the idea of a geologic column does not in and of itself contain any assumption about the age of the earth, only the composition of its crust. The calculation of the age of the earth which Darwin relied upon in his book was in fact based totally upon the works of Charles Lyell and James Hutton. As we have already seen, both of these men absolutely rejected catastrophic occurrences as plausible explanations for the geologic formations we see around us today.[40] Accordingly, Darwin reasoned that any fossil found in a rock formation Lyell estimated to be half a billion years old must itself be half a billion years old. Were it not for the anticatastrophic viewpoint held by Lyell and Hutton, Darwin would have had *no basis* for assuming that any formation was anywhere near as old as half a billion years.

Since Lyell's calculations were not based upon Darwin's theory, upon what then was his anticatastrophic theory of uniformitarianism based? *Absolutely nothing!* Nothing, that is, except his reasoning that since he had never seen a worldwide deluge, none had ever occurred. We can now begin to see the intellectual problem facing the evolutionists. If Lyell was wrong, then there was no valid reason for Darwin to have assumed that his fossil discoveries were ancient, because Darwin's concept of the age of the earth was based solely upon Lyell's now discredited theory. At this point the problem which the evolutionists have created for themselves comes into full focus. What evolutionists must now maintain is a position which goes something like this: "Both Lyell and Darwin were correct in all their ultimate conclusions, but they were right for all the wrong reasons." Putting it another way they could say, "Both Darwin and Lyell arrived at the correct destination, but they took all the wrong roads to get there." Not only are we expected to accept this type of evolutionistic thought process as scientific, but they want us to do so in spite of the fact that two of their foundational premises have been abandoned by their most prominent spokesmen.

Eldredge states that "geologists *long ago* abandoned... [the idea] that all changes in earth history were the product of infinitesimally minute changes gradually accumulating through time."[41] This contention that the anticatastrophic portions of Lyell's theory were abandoned by geologists *long ago* is however contradicted by the America Geological Society[42]:

[T]hey [geologists] learned that the features of the earth's surface could be adequately accounted for by *cumulative processes*, operating not only in the past, but in the visible present. The valleys of the earth, they found were *not torn open by violent paroxysms* of the planet's surface, but were *slowly excavated* by running water over *immense periods of time*....

Even as late as 1985 the *World Book Encyclopedia*[43] was informing its readers that "[G]eologists base their explanations of rock clues on their observations of the earth today.... . Geologists also assume that the earth has developed in the past in the same way as it is developing now. This idea "first proposed by James Hutton...is now called the principle of uniformitarianism." I therefore submit that if in fact this aspect of Lyell's uniformitarianism theory has been abandoned by some modern evolutionists, it was not done so long ago, but only recently. Even then it was abandoned not because it is clearly wrong, but because they feel that they no longer need it.

You see, they have discovered something else which seems to give them the billions of years they need for their theory. These new techniques of calculating age appear to have a more scientific basis than did Lyell's hypothesis. Had it not been for the radioisotope dating methods developed in the late 1950's and early 1960's, evolutionists would still be clinging tenaciously to Lyell's anticatastrophic views, even though they had no basis in fact when Lyell developed them. Recognizing the fact that Lyell's position was totally baseless, modern evolutionists have in effect acknowledged that Lyell was wrong.

We are now faced with a situation similar to that which we saw in the case of Darwin's gradualism. First of all, today's crop of evolutionists are again telling us that something which we had been assured was as much a scientific fact as gravity is not a fact at all. In reality, "anticatastrophic geologic uniformitarianism" is nothing more than another now thoroughly discredited evolutionistic fairy tale. Secondly, and perhaps most disturbing to me, is the fact that "the nineteenth century idea of uniformitarianism and gradualism still exists in popular treatments of geology, some museum exhibits, and in lower level textbooks. It is even still taught in secondary school classrooms."[49]

Again, our school children are being exposed to evolutionary myth and then being assured that it is a scientific fact. This is in spite of the fact that Lyell's anticatastrophic view point was not the result of a simple oversight on his behalf. In order for Lyell to arrive at his position he had to actually ignore the very evidence which should have told him he was wrong. According to at least one noted evolutionist, Lyell and other 19th century geologists had to "ignore or give very secondary importance" to the many examples of geologic catastrophism which they themselves discovered.[45]

It should be noted concerning the interrelationships which existed between Lyell's version of geology and Darwin's version of biology that Eldredge maintains that there isn't any: "Geologists on the whole don't care a fig about evolution—*haven't in the past*, and as far as I can tell still don't care much about it today."[46] I believe that Eldredge has made this statement in an attempt to prove that both geologists and biologists scientifically arrived at the same conclusion that the earth is billions of years old and that they did so independently of each other.

However, the noted British geologist Sir Archibald Geikie clearly contradicted this assertion when he stated in 1910 that "[T]he publication of Darwin's *Origin of the*

Species...produced an extraordinary revolution in geological opinion. The older schools of thought rapidly died out and evolution became the recognized creed of geologists all over the world."[47] Even today "fossils help geologists figure out the ages of rock strata..."[48] Enough has been said for now about the age of the rocks and the fossils found in them. I will discuss this topic in greater detail a little later on.

As we return to the concept of uniformitarianism, allow me to ask several questions. What forces of nature today are moving individual mountains from Africa to Switzerland? What forces of nature are producing fossils of the type discovered by Leakey (or any type for that matter)? When you find out, please tell his son, for in regard to the soft-bodied fossils Leakey discovered prior to his death he stated, "How did these incredible fossils occur? We simply do not know."[49] The incongruity of the evolutionists' thought process becomes more apparent.

Evolutionists first make the assumption that any god who created the universe must not be working today. They then state that the forces of nature at work today are sufficient to explain everything that happened in the past. Then they turn around and say that they do not know what forces of nature created the very fossils upon which they have to depend as they try to prove their theory. They also ignore the overwhelming exceptions to the arbitrary rules they themselves have set up when it is pointed out to them that their rules violate the rules of true science. Needless to say, not much is said in high school textbooks about all the exceptions we have just examined. In fact, these books usually leave the impression that everything in nature follows the evolutionists' pattern.

Here are a few other questions which need to be asked: What forces of nature at work today produced the Deccan Plateau of India which is composed of over a million square miles of lava sometimes thousands of feet thick? What forces of nature at work today explain how the quarter-million-square-mile Utah-Arizona plateau apparently rose from below sea level to a mile above sea level, as many evolutionistic geologists say it did, without disturbing the relatively even distribution of marine fossils found in the strata which this plateau comprises? What forces of nature at work today explain islands which contain fossilized land animals submerged 6 thousand feet below the surface of the ocean?

Dr. K.K. Landes, chairman of the department of geology at the University of Michigan, asked this question of his fellow geologists: "Can we, as seekers after the truth, shut our eyes any longer to the fact that large areas of sea floor have sunk vertical distances measured in miles?"[50] I submit that open-minded scientists who carefully follow their own rules of hypothesis and testing and who are open to change are not ignoring such problems. However, most evolutionists appear to have the habit of doing exactly what Stephen Gould said they do, that is, if it doesn't fit their theory, they simply do not talk about it.

But Dr. Gould's candid statement which was quoted near the beginning of this chapter is not the only one we have to substantiate the charge that evolutionists have a habit of ignoring the facts which are overwhelmingly in conflict with their theory. Dr. Robert Jastrow, director of NASA's Goddard Institute for Space Studies noted that

Astronomers are curiously upset by...proof that the universe had a beginning. Their reactions provide an interesting demonstration of the response of the scientific mind—supposedly a very objective mind—when evidence uncovered by science itself leads to a conflict with the articles of faith in their profession.... . There is a kind of religion in science; a faith that every event can be explained as the product of some previous event.... . This conviction is violated by the discovery that the world had a beginning under conditions in which the known laws of physics are not valid...the scientist has lost control. If he really examined the implications he would be traumatized. *As usual, when the mind is faced with trauma, it reacts by ignoring the implications.*[51]

However, we should not be so naive as to believe that all this absent-mindedness is trauma induced. Pierre-Paul Grassé, past president of the French Académie des Sciences and himself an evolutionist, candidly noted that

The deceit is sometimes unconscious, *but not always*, since some people, owing to their sectarianism, purposefully overlook reality and refuse to acknowledge the inadequacies and the falsity of their beliefs.[52]

Other evolutionists have been known to ignore the evidence facing them for reasons which are decidedly less lofty than philosophical ones. Again, you need not take my word alone in order to substantiate this point. While giving the 1980 assembly week address at the University of Melbourne, Professor Whitten, a member of the genetics department who even though holding to the evolutionists' position pointed out that

Biologists are simply naive when they talk about experiments designed to test the theory of evolution. It is not testable. They may happen to stumble across facts which would seem to conflict with its predictions. *These facts will invariably be ignored and their discoverers will undoubtedly be deprived of continuing research grants.*[53]

By no means could the prominent biologists S. Lovtrup, professor of zoophysiology at the University of Umeå in Sweden, be considered a creationist. Yet, he too has observed the fact that Darwinian evolutionists regularly ignore the facts which disprove their theory. As he points out, this is not merely a recent phenomenon. He states,

...the Darwinian theory of natural selection, whether or not coupled with Mendelism, is false... . [T]here are now considerable numbers of empirical facts which do not fit with the theory. Hence, to all intents and purposes the theory has been falsified, so why is it not abandoned? I think the answer to this question is that current evolutionists *following Darwin's example— they refuse to accept falsifying evidence.*[54]

It would appear that the evolutionist's mind is a perfect example of the principle that if we hold unsound presuppositions with sufficient tenacity facts will make no difference at all.

Many evolutionists hold on to the uniformitarianism theory because it is one of the few concepts which gives them the billions of years they need to work with. However, if consistently applied, it presents innumerably more problems to them than it apparently solves. For example, sediment formed by microscopic marine organisms and dust blown or washed into the ocean should have blanketed the sea floor to a uniform depth of at least 12 miles if in fact the earth is even half as old as evolutionists maintain. Yet, none is found in the center of the Atlantic and only a half-mile-thick veneer is found along the continental shelf.[55] Furthermore, assuming that salt is being added to the ocean today at a rate no greater than it has in the past and even assuming that there was no salt in the oceans at their inception, the salinity of the oceans demands a date for their creation of not more than 200 thousand years ago. That is at least 3 billion years younger than any evolutionists can accept.

Finally, we also know from observation and testing that iron meteorites strike the earth at a given rate per year. If in fact the geologic formations of the earth were laid down over a period of several billion years, then it would be easy to find tons of iron meteorites in each layer of sediment. Whereas if these layers were set down over a very short period (say one year or less), such as would have been the case in the biblical flood, then few, if any, would be found in the middle or lower layers. The fact that *no* iron meteorites have been found in the so-called ancient geologic layers is merely one more traumatic fact which many evolutionists simply forget to mention in their writings.[56]

The foregoing points are all ignored, glossed over, minimized as to their import, or given explanations which are totally untestable and then passed off as factual when they many times are in direct conflict with the "scientific" facts the evolutionists wanted us to believe only a few short years ago. Yet, there are even greater examples of the evolutionists' ignoring the very laws of true science to which they supposedly subscribe. Some of them can be shown as we examine their concept of how our solar system developed.

Chapter 3

Real Science Has Its Say

According to one of the more prominent currently acceptable theories, the planets in our solar system were spun off from the sun. Each planet was flung into space where it cooled and now revolves around the sun. However, if this is true, why do the planets rotate around their axes faster than the sun rotates around its own—in violation of the rules governing centrifugal force? Why do Uranus and Venus rotate on their axes in a direction opposite that of the other seven planets if they were spun off from the same sun? Why do planets with moons, except Earth, rotate faster than their moons? Why do 11 of the 32 moons revolve around their planets in a direction opposite that in which the planets revolve around the sun? Finally, if Earth were formed from the sun, which is 99 percent hydrogen, how did its heavy elements such as iron and nickel develop? The theory of neutron capture does not appear to be a satisfactory explanation, because it does not adequately account for the problem of overcoming the instability of those elements with an atomic mass number of 5 or 8. You see, you cannot build on these unstable elements unless other elements with higher numbers are already present. In effect, they are the weak links in the chain.

It must be pointed out however that in addition to all of the above inconsistencies, there is one other law of true science which the entire theory of evolution absolutely and unequivocally violates, that is, the second law of thermodynamics, more commonly referred to as entropy. This law states in effect that all natural processes lead to an increase in the randomness of the system being considered. *Things left to themselves to be operated on by chance do not get more and more organized, but rather more and more disorganized.* It doesn't say things first get more complicated and then eventually less so; it says "more and more disorganized."

By definition, evolution is an idea which demands two things: first, chance happenings and second, a progression from the simple to the complex. That puts evolution in direct conflict with one of the most accepted of all the laws of true science. The only defense to this objection which evolutionists give is a smoke screen which goes something like this: What could be more natural than the growth of a human being from the time that the egg is fertilized until death. It grows, becoming more complicated, and then it gets old, less complicated, and dies, thereby succumbing to the law of entropy.

Evolutionists use this false example to allow for the intervening stage of complexity. This however is quite misleading, as entropy operates only on a system which is left to itself to be operated on by chance. The growth of a human being from embryo to adulthood is not controlled by random chance, but by the programmed chromosomes we received from our parents. But we should not be surprised by misleading examples because, as we will see a little later on in this study, outright hoaxes as well as misleading statements have played an important part in the development of the theory of evolution.

Not only does Darwinian evolution violate the second law of thermodynamics, but what has been long hailed by evolutionists themselves as the best example of evolution actually violates the very theory it is supposed to prove. I am referring to the famous horse example. Eldredge states, "...the fossil record is full of examples of progressive changes (from ancestor into descendant). Horses to take but one, got larger... ."[1] The 1972 edition of *Encyclopedia Britannica* states that the "horse family has the most complete fossil record of any group of mammals." (See also World Book Encyclopedia, Vol. 8, 1985 ed., p. 326.) Why there are not also "complete" records of the evolution of all those mammals which are far more numerous than horses is another question which the evolutionists seem to ignore. But that is not the issue I wish to discuss here, so I will merely allow you to ponder that one for yourself.

According to the evolutionary horse theory, our modern horse evolved gradually from the now extinct eohippus, a 28-inch-tall, multitoed mammal. But here is the problem with that theory. Evolution says things change from the less complex to the more complex, from the weak to the strong. But this prime example fails to comply with the evolutionary theory's own premise in at least three major areas. First, a more complex, four-toed mammal (with three toes on the hind quarter) "evolved" into a less complex one-toed horse. Secondly, a strong, arch-backed eohippus "evolved" into the much weaker, straight-backed or sway-backed horse. Thirdly, the eohippus had more teeth than the modern horse. Each of these observations provide a clear example of the more complex "evolving" into the less complex, and that is not evolution, but deterioration.

Furthermore, the charts and drawings used to illustrate this supposed change are unfair in that they generally show the smallest known eohippus, about 27 inches high, alongside the largest modern horse. They do not show us that there were several species of *eohippus* which were about the size of a Shetland pony and at least one modern breed of horse that is only 29 inches tall. This distortion of what the fossil record actually does reveal concerning the horse family is so outrageous that even Heribert Nilsson, a prominent European evolutionist has conceded that "[t]he family tree of the horse is *beautiful and continuous only in the textbooks.*"[2] Finally, the evolutionists who write the textbooks and encyclopedia articles which almost always cite the horse example as proof for their theory somehow forget to acknowledge the fact that David M. Raup, formerly of the Field Museum of Natural History in Chicago and currently associated with the University of Chicago, among other noted evolutionists, has stated that "[s]ince the time of Darwin we have just as many gaps as before...a few we thought had been filled in, *like the horse series, are now known to be wrong.*"[3]

There are still other areas which the evolutionists regularly fail to discuss, and a careful examination of them will give us a better understanding of why it is statistically impossible for evolution to be a plausible explanation for the origin of life as we know it. For example, if we use the evolutionists' own date of about 1 million years ago for the initial appearance of man and if population growth had continued in the past at a rate equal to only one-fourth its current rate of two percent per year, humans would be so numerous that we would literally pack the universe. For those who claim that this would be impossible because of the lack of modern medicine and the outbreak of plagues, I suggest that you consider the fact that prior to the appearance of comparatively modern medicine in 1600 A.D., world population was growing at a rate far in excess of .5 percent per annum. Also, plagues would not have been a major problem until the population had become somewhat concentrated, and there is no evidence of such concentration before the Middle Ages. On the other hand, if we take the current level of the world's population and its growth rate and then calculate backward in time, we would be down to approximately eight people by the date Archbishop Ussher determined to be the biblical flood using the chronologies found in the Bible.[4]

Another statistical problem which is not mentioned very often is one which I am certain that most of us have not even considered. Evolutionists invoke astronomically huge numbers not because they want to, but because they have to in order to bring the odds of something happening as they insist it must have into a more mathematically acceptable range of possibility. Think about this for a moment. Evolutionists tells us that plant life evolved over a period of literally hundreds of millions of years. They also tell us that insect life evolved over a similarly long period of time. Considering the extreme complexity of both the plant and insect kingdoms, even that time span does not appear to be long enough. However, now evolutionists are asking us to believe that certain events coincided to such an extent that over all those eons of time the fig tree and the wasp not only evolved into their present forms by sheer chance, but they did so *simultaneously*. They want us to accept the notion that in the spring of the same year they reached that point of evolution where the fig tree could only be pollinated by the wasp, and the wasp coincidentally acquired the ability or inclination to pollinate the fig. The fact that both things had to have happened simultaneously more than doubles the statistical odds necessary for either event to have happened separately.

There are many other examples of such symbiotic relationships in nature. Each one further compounds the mathematical improbabilities which the evolutionist must overcome if his theory is to have even the slightest chance of working out as he says it does. We have mentioned the statistical problem involved in the *relatively simple* process of fig pollination, let us now turn our attention to the much more complex question of animal reproduction.

In the case of evolutionary asexual reproduction what had to have happened was not only the chance development of a simple cell, but a "simple" cell which also had within itself the ability to reproduce. In and of itself that statistically complicates the whole matter by astounding proportions Yet, the problem for the evolutionist only increases as we move from simple cell division to sexual reproduction.

Concerning such reproduction, we have to assume that both male and female reproductive organs, with all their intricacies, appeared at the same time. If we do not make such an assumption, the evolutionist is faced with two insurmountable problems. First, how did animals reproduce sexually even at the lowest levels of life, if total development were not complete? Secondly, even if they did manage to reproduce in some nonsexual or asexual manner, we must assume that they had organs or portions of organs developing over eons which would not be used until all the parts necessary for sexual reproduction came into being. This however would be a violation of another evolutionary concept called "natural selection." According to this concept, nature acting by itself will eliminate that which is not used. Thus, the individual reproductive organs would be eliminated by natural selection before the other organs evolved, unless of course *all* the organs necessary for reproduction in both males and females "evolved" at the same instant. No wonder the evolutionists need billions of years to try to get things to work out just right. They have to overcome the statistical improbabilities of these events occurring as they say they did.

The theory of punctuated equilibria compounds the matter even more. According to this theory, we are expected to believe that even greater changes occurred over a shorter span of time in the majority of all species. But evolutionists not only overlook this problem, they totally ignore the final mathematical mountain they face, i.e., it is a *statistical impossibility* for all the hard-shell and soft-bodied organisms which are found in the Cambrian rock formation and which are acknowledged to have appeared simultaneously to have done so by chance in even the 4 billion years which evolutionists maintain is the outside estimate of age for the earth.[5]

Even after all that is settled in his mind, the evolutionist is faced with the fact that the virus, the *simplest* of all known living organisms, will grow *only* in or on living cells of higher life forms. Furthermore, if we assume that scientists (not evolutionists, but scientists) would be able to reproduce basic life forms under laboratory conditions, evolution will not have been proved. What would be proved is that thousands of human beings working in numerous laboratories throughout the world with the most sophisticated equipment could produce simple life forms. In other words, they would prove that intelligent beings can bring forth life, something any Christian could tell them from reading Genesis chapters 1 and 2.

But they are a long, long, long way from producing any forms of life. (Amino acids produced in a laboratory are not living matter.) Part of the reason for this lack of success is that the so-called simple cell is anything but simple. In fact, the complications presented by the very existence of DNA and RNA in simple cells are such that no evolutionary biologist has yet had the courage to insist that we accept as fact the notion that DNA molecules are definitely chance happenings which evolved from what ultimately must have been some type of inorganic matter.

Why won't they make such an absurd allegation? It is simple. Once you get past the whole issue of spontaneous generation (which Louis Pasteur was finally able to put to rest in the 1800's), the chances of even the first rung of DNA structure being reached randomly are 10 to the 87th power. That's 10 followed by 87 zeros, which could be translated to about 7 billion years. Not even the most ardent evolutionists are willing to take on the job of convincing anyone that it took close to 7 billion years for even the first single-cell life form to emerge from what can only be described as primordial slime.[6]

But DNA does not work by itself. It works only if 20 different proteins also are there to perform their functions, but these proteins only work at the direction of DNA. Since each requires the other to operate, a satisfactory explanation for the origin of one must of necessity also explain the origin of the other. As in the case of the fig tree and the wasp, the relationship between DNA and these 20 proteins more than doubles the statistical odds of either one developing separately by random chance.

So much for the single-cell organism. What about the cells of more highly developed life forms? Each nucleus of every cell in the human body contains 23 pairs of chromosomes which were inherited from our parents. If these 46 chromosomes were placed end to end, they would form a chain seven feet long (although it would be so thin that you couldn't see it even with an electron microscope). The information coded on that chain would be enough to fill over 4 thousand average size books. What's more, each cell in the human body—all 30 trillion of them—contains this identical information.[7] In addition we need to consider the following: While all the DNA material found in the average adult could fit into a space no bigger than an ice cube, if each strand in that cube were joined end to end, it would reach from the earth to the sun and back *more than four hundred times.*[8] However, we are expected by evolutionists to believe that all this somehow evolved by chance from nonliving matter!

The whole topic of DNA and the long-term implications it holds for the theory of evolution could be the subject of a separate book in and of itself. However, I would be guilty of a gross oversight if I didn't at least touch upon one other point regarding DNA. This discussion will serve two purposes: First, it will again highlight the evolutionists' tendency to ignore the facts which disprove their theory. Second, it destroys a third major tenent of the evolutionary concept. This tenent holds that man evolved simultaneously in different parts of the world. In the words of Richard Leakey in 1977, "There is no single center where modern man was born."[9]

Anthropologists who hold to such a position as Leakey's are now faced with a serious problem. According to an article which appeared in the January 11, 1988, issues of *Newsweek* magazine, "...a new breed of anthropologists...[t]rained in molecular biology...picked up a trail of DNA that led them to a *single woman from which we are all descendants*... [H]ers seems to be in all humans living today."[10] Geneticists have in effect proved what Genesis 1:27 has been telling us all along, "...modern humans didn't slowly and inexorably evolve in different parts of the world."[11] In fact, the evidence for this new discovery is so compelling that Stephen Jay Gould now acknowledges that "all human beings despite difference in external appearance are really members of a *single entity* that's had a very *recent origin in one place*."[12] The evolutionists are unwilling to accept a date for this occurrence which is less than 200 thousand years ago, but that is a far cry from the dates and places they previously insisted upon as *fact*.

One of the geneticists who made these discoveries back in 1967, Dr. Alan Wilson, acknowledges that there were probably no more than a "few thousand" members of this woman's generation living on the face of the earth at the time she lived.[13] While scientists will not concede that this woman was the first woman on earth or the only one at the time, they also cannot totally dismiss the possibility that that is exactly who she was.

During the past few years questions have been raised concerning the computer programming techniques employed by the geneticists engaged in this study. Some scientists have even questioned the entire validity of this project because of these techniques. However, the results of this study have been confirmed by an even more comprehensive study conducted in 1991. The results of this verification study are so conclusive that the geneticists who conducted it have stated that the odds favoring the single-ancestor theory are now 16 thousand to one.[14] In other words, there appears to be little doubt in the minds of most researchers that all people alive today came from a single woman who most likely originated in the vicinity of Africa or the Middle East.

Traditional evolutionists also questioned the validity of the original study; however, they did so not for scientific reasons, but simply because it conflicted with their preconceived notions about the origin of man. The point is, this study was initially denounced not because of any supposed flaw in its technique, but solely because of the contradictory nature of its findings. Such reasoning represents the very antithesis of true science.

In regard to our supposed primate ancestry, many evolutionists still insist that the human line split off from that of the chimpanzee about 15 million years ago. Geneticists though have proved that this simply cannot be so. The difference in the molecular structure of a particular blood protein in chimps and humans is so small that they could not possibly have gone their separate way any more than 5 million years ago. (Remember, the evolutionists' denial of a Creator God forces them to see similarity in design not as evidence for a designer, but as evidence for evolution.) The point is, as *Newsweek* reported, "Traditional anthropologists did not appreciate being told that their estimates were off...by ten million years. The geneticists' calculation was *dismissed and ignored* for more than a decade."[15]

Richard Leakey, while having no formal education beyond high school, was trained by his father Louis Leakey to know how to "organize an expedition and...to find fossils."[16] He represents one type of traditional anthropologist who spends his time in "desiccated African rift valley[s]" looking for bones, as opposed to the more laboratory-bound molecular biologists who have disproved the simultaneous appearance theory.[17] Yet, the concern even of many of Leakey's more academically accredited "stones and bones" colleagues appears to be more closely related to their image than to their 10-million-year mistake: "What bothers many of us paleontologists," said Fred Smith of the University of Tennessee, "is the perception that this new data from DNA is so precise and scientific and that we paleontologists are just a bunch of bumbling old fools...we may be bumbling fools, but we're not any more bumbling than they [the geneticists] are."[18]

Because of the insurmountable problems faced by the evolutionists, such as the ones we have just examined, 52 of the world's top mathematicians and evolutionists met at Wistar Institute in Philadelphia, Pennsylvania, to analyze the mathematical problems presented by the so-called scientific theory of evolution. After computer-assisted analysis of all the data, they came to the conclusion that evolution was a mathematical impossibility. Dr. Murray Eden of the Massachusetts Institute of Technology stated, "So great were the problems, that before we could have a viable theory of evolution there would have to be the discovery and illucidation of entirely new natural laws; chemical, chemical/physical, and biological."[19] Why did Dr. Eden make such a statement? The theory of evolution violates virtually all of the known laws of true science.

Even all this has not stopped the intrepid evolutionist from continuing to push his "scientific" theory. Now however it takes on more of the characteristics of science fiction than science. With but one notable exception, evolutionists can state only that the origins of DNA and RNA, like the sudden appearance of all those Cambrian multicellular life forms, are a mystery. That exception is the suggestion by Nobel prizewinner Francis Crick that simple life forms originated somewhere else and came to earth by unknown means.[20] Needless to say, from the scientific perspective this "it came from outer space" idea (otherwise known as directed aspermiai) leaves a great deal to be desired. First of all, like many other evolutionistic concepts, it is totally untestable. Secondly, by shifting the location of life's mysterious appearance from the earth to some other planet in some other solar system, the evolutionists is hoping that you will not notice that this explanation still does not explain *how* simple cells appeared. (Crick's theory is a perfect example of an infinite regression which directs the reader's attention backward, but never actually answers the original question.)

Think about this for a moment. Why would it even be logical to assume that a life form so well suited to Earth would have had a better chance of evolving on some other planet which must have had an identical atmosphere to that of Earth's and then survived the journey to Earth on some asteroid or meteor?

When you think of it, the theory of the origin of the species known as Darwinian evolution actually has a very poor record of explaining origins. As we have seen so far, the origins of basic molecules such as DNA and RNA and the sudden origins of Cambrian multicellular life forms are each classified as mysteries. But then from the evolutionists' standpoint, this is as it must be, for not one single piece of evidence exists among the fossil collections in all the museums of the world to prove that the origins were evolutionary in nature.

Evolutionists however have not limited their use of science fiction to explanations which deal with the appearance of lower life forms. While it is true that Richard Goldschmidt of the University of California at Berkeley was one of the first academicians to publicly mention the fact that the fossil record simply did not support the notion that there were transitions between higher-category life forms, it must be remembered that he was first and foremost an evolutionist. Therefore, rather than accept the fact that the fossil record does support the concept of special creation, Goldschmidt proposed an hypothesis which became known as the theory of the "hopeful monster."[21]

Since no graduated transitional forms could be discovered, Goldschmidt rightly assumed that none had ever existed. To explain the "leap" from reptiles to birds he relied upon the concept of mutations. Even though it can be seen from simple observation that the vast majority of all genetic mutations are harmful, he assumed that within one generation there must have been literally hundreds of beneficial mutations which resulted in a higher life form. In effect, he was saying that when a lizard laid an egg, a particular lizard embryo had virtually every one of its organs altered by massive genetic mutations. When this egg hatched, what emerged was not a funny-looking lizard, but a fully developed bird!

Chapter 4

Oops, Sorry About That

As we have just mentioned the topic of biological organs in the previous chapter, allow me to briefly discuss what else we can expect from what is in reality not the science of evolution, but the philosophy/religion of evolution. The topic of vestigial organs points out the evolutionists' tendency to grab at every shred of supposed evidence that seems to support their theory and then assure us, "That is the way it was!" A vestigial organ is an organ which evolutionists claim served some useful function somewhere down the evolutionary line, but which no longer is useful to the creature in which it is found. Biologists discovered early in their research about 180 organs in the human being for which they could find no purpose. Evolutionists were quick to claim that these "vestigial" organs supported their theory.[1] They pointed out that since some of these same organs were found to be more highly developed in some lower life forms, additional proof of evolution had been established.

The *Encyclopedia Britannica* carries this line of reasoning when it reports that evolutionists believe that "animals that have the same organ in a fully developed and functional condition are believed to be close to the ancestry of the animal having the vestigial organ."[2] While that may sound scientific, here is where we begin to see part of the fallacy of the evolutionists' reasoning. Using their logic it is possible to deduce that a man is more closely related to the koala bear (which is a marsupial) and the rabbit, than he is to the great apes. You see, apes generally do not have an appendix whereas both koala bears and rabbits have fully developed ones. Since man's appendix is supposedly left over from his evolutionary development, it is therefore obvious that we are more closely related to "Bugs Bunny" than to the primates.

Once again true science has come to rescue us from such a ridiculous set of circumstances, and once again the evolutionists have been proven wrong. True scientists have discovered that of the 180 organs whose functions were previously unexplainable, many have been found to produce necessary hormones. Several function only during the embryonic stage of human development, and some only in emergencies—coming on line, as it were, only when the primary system fails. Many biologists now feel that the functions of the few remaining unexplained organs will reveal themselves as research continues. In the meantime, what were supposedly vestigial organs have not proven evolution, but have reaffirmed in greater detail the complexity of God's final creation—mankind.

One further example of the evolutionists' use of a biological process as an absurd "proof" of evolution deals with the infamous concept known as the recapitulation theory. According to this notion, the human embryo, from the moment the egg is fertilized until its development is completed, passes through stages which reflect every stage of man's evolutionary process from single-cell life form to fish to amphibian to mammal and, finally to primate. They have referred to this by saying that "ontogeny recapitulates [repeats] phylogeny." Darwin continually referred to this notion in both his *Origin of the Species* and *Descent of Man,* and it has been used by numerous evolutionists ever since.

Their use of this idea is foolish at best and spurious at worst because, as noted by Yale University professor of biology Dr. Keith Thompson, "...as a topic of serious theoretical inquiry, it was *extinct in the twenties.*"[3] Tragically, however, this false proof for evolution didn't disappear from biology textbooks until the late 1940's.[4] For almost 30 years the evolutionists were teaching as "fact" something which had already been dismissed as intellectually meaningless.

Even today it is not beyond an evolutionist to try to resurrect this long-dead theory in a futile attempt to prove his theory, as did Dr. Anthony Wheeler during a debate at the University of Queensland, Brisbane, Australia, on March 30, 1988.[5] The popular press is just as guilty of perpetrating this fraud. The August 1990 issue of *Life* magazine stated that a six-week human embryo displays characteristics which demonstrate "*a strong link with an animal past.*"[6] Remember now, this statement has been made in spite of the fact that there has not been even a hint of scientific justification to substantiate it for more than half a century!

A more interesting example of the evolutionists' willingness to accept anything that comes along are the fossil remains given the very impressive scientific name *Eoanthropus dawsoni.* These fossils, found in 1913, for more than 40 years were given the status within the evolutionary community as the second most important fossil find to establish the evolutionary heritage of mankind.[7] Yet, the Piltdown Man, as he was commonly called, was eventually discovered to be a deliberate hoax. After more than four decades of misleading the public, evolutionists flippantly dismissed this hoax as merely "evidence of skullduggery in the ranks of academia," but they do not mention the total failure of the "evolutionary scientists" to notice the hoax.[8] As late as February 1953, writers such as Ruth Moore who had swallowed the evolutionists line were still assuring the general public that the Piltdown Man was "the first modern man."[9] It's a shame that Ms. Moore did not wait nine more months before publishing her book, because on November 21, 1953, the British scientific community finally exposed the Piltdown skull for what it really was, namely, one more piece of phoney evolutionistic evidence.[10]

Even this did not deter them. Evolutionists have been so anxious to prove their theory that they even hailed the discovery of a single tooth and gave it the even more impressive name *Hesperopithecus haroldcooki.* Using their preconceived notions of what he must have looked like and this single tooth, the undaunted "scientists" who gave credence to the Piltdown Man now gave us the Nebraska Man. Unfortunately for them, the tooth upon which this "man" was built turned out to be that of a pig! The highly scientific explanation for this *mistake* given by one evolutionist on behalf of his colleagues was, "...pig and human molars are rather similar."[11] Keep in mind that this excuse was given in an attempt to explain why so-called thoughtful, unbiased, thorough, and detail-minded evolutionistic scientists could not distinguish the molar of an extinct pig from that of a higher primate.

This excuse rings even more hollow when we consider the fact that the discoverer of this tooth, Harold J. Cook, had earlier coauthored an article with W.D. Matthew wherein they warned other evolutionists to be careful when dealing with the teeth of these now extinct pigs.[12] The point is Cook and Matthew were clearly put on notice to proceed with caution, as were their colleagues Henry Fairfield Osborn and William King Gregory, to whom they had sent the tooth. However, in what can only be described as an effort to gain glory and at the same time attack the credibility of William Jennings Bryan, the noted creationists attorney who was from the state of Nebraska, Osborn threw all caution to the wind. He proceeded with his irresponsible declaration that man's supposed ancestor had been discovered in Bryan's home state.[13]

One further example of the evolutionists' rush to judgment is provided by the fossil remains of what became known as Neanderthal Man. The first fossil remains of this man were described as belonging to a creature who "walked with his knees permanently bent, his arms reaching forward, and his head thrust out on a short slanting neck." In fact, every picture or statue of Neanderthal Man which appeared before 1955 in any evolutionary textbook or in any museum depicted a hunched over primate that appeared to be some from of transition between man and ape.

In order to ensure the apelike appearance of its Neanderthal wax model, one American museum even spent thousands of dollars having human hair implanted all over its body. Remember now, this was done even though we had absolutely no way of telling anything about the color of Neanderthal's skin, his hair or eye color, or the type or abundance of his hair.[15] Not only that, but most evolutionists now admit that if you were to put Neanderthal Man in a suit, he would go about completely unnoticed in the subway or supermarket.[16]

Needless to say, there is a vast difference between the image which comes to mind when we think of a hunched-over, hairy primate and that of the gentleman in the gray flannel suit, which he so easily could have been. This misconception concerning his appearance started when the first fossils of Neanderthal Man were found in 1856, and it was reinforced by additional discoveries by the French anatomist/ paleontologist, Marcellin Boule in 1911. It was not until about 1955, almost 100 years later, that a *careful* examination of those fossils showed that the man to whom they belonged suffered from a crippling case of rickets and also possibly arthritis. After all the pictures had been changed and all the old statues replaced with ones which depicted a fully upright Neanderthal Man, the previous *oversight* was quickly forgotten. No mention is made by evolutionists of the fact that for almost 100 years our parents, grandparents, and in some cases our great-grandparents were assured that it was a "scientific fact" that Neanderthal Man was hunched over and apelike in appearance, when this simply was not true.

In each of the above-mentioned cases, further research, study, and investigation eventually exposed the evolutionists' rush to judgment, but not before many young minds had been exposed to the travesty represented by evolutionistic "science." As we shall now see, the fossilized remains of humans present overwhelming problems for the evolutionists' theory, even when they aren't tampered with.

Niles Eldredge maintains that "creationists fare poorly in the face of the tremendous amount of well publicized information about the human fossil record."[17] However, when you consider that the evolutionists' track record includes Piltdown Man, Nebraska Man, Neanderthal man, and a few other blunders which I haven't even discussed, I don't see how anyone could say that they have succeeded in their quest to prove man's evolutionary heritage. A fair question to ask at this point would be, "Exactly how extensive is the fossil record which supposedly proves man's evolutionary heritage?"

According to the noted anthropologist Dr. Lyall Watson, "The remarkable fact is that all the physical evidence we have for human evolution can still be placed, with room to spare, inside a single coffin."[18] Aside from the fact that this is a most fitting place in which to store the supposed evidence of man's evolutionary past, Watson makes it clear that, as we have so often seen before, the evolutionists' case rests more on wishful thinking than on hard evidence. As noted by a science correspondent for *U.S. News and World Report*, even as late as February 1989 the evolutionists' depiction of human development had been "...rendered with a *dab of science* and a *bucketful of speculation*, [and was] [b]ased as much on *wishful thinking* or intellectual fashion as the scanty fossil evidence left by our ancestors."[19] Photo journalist John Reader carries this thought one step further. Having first observed that "[t]he entire hominid [fossil] collection known today would barely cover a billiard table," Reader pointed out the fact that the "specimens themselves [are] often so fragmentary and inconclusive, that more can be said about what is missing than about what is present."[20]

When evolutionists like Dr. Tim White, an anthropologist at the University of California at Berkeley, honestly survey their field, they acknowledge that "[t]he problem with a lot of anthropologists is that they want so much to find a hominid that any scrap of bone becomes a hominid bone."[21] (It should be noted here that White's statement was taken from an article in *New Scientist* which had been written to explain why some evolutionists had mistaken a dolphin rib for an ancient hominid collarbone!)

Furthermore, if the comparatively minute amount of human fossil "evidence" is not sufficient to discourage evolutionists, the most recent discoveries of Donald C. Johanson and Richard Leakey have done as much to disprove the theory of evolution as anything we have seen lately in the area of anthropology. While I most certainly do not accept the ages which evolutionists claim for their discoveries, I am going to refer to them because they have again painted themselves into a corner with their own words.

According to Johanson, both modern men and modern apes developed along parallel lines. Each line sprang from a common ancestor about 3.8 million years ago. The scientific classification assigned to this ancestor is *Australopithecus afarensis*. More commonly known as "Lucy," this creature was about 3.5 feet tall and had long arms and long curved fingers and toes. (It should be noted here that long arms and long curved fingers and toes are anatomical features used for swinging from branches.[23]) On July 21, 1986, Johanson uncovered some additional fossils which he classified as *Homo habilis* (handyman). In spite of the fact that these fossils reveal a creature who was 3 feet tall (6 inches shorter than Lucy) with long arms and long curved fingers and toes and a skeletal structure which was just as primitive as Lucy's, these fossils were placed immediately below true man in the evolutionary chain. Perhaps these fossils were placed there by Johanson because he believes that they were only 1.8 millions years old.[24] Their reported age and assigned position in the evolutionists' time chart means that 2 million years transpired without any noticeable change taking place between Lucy and her direct descendants. This however is not the main problem facing evolutionists today in regard to these fossils.

In 1984 Richard Leakey found the full skeleton of a 12-year-old boy who was already 5 feet 4 inches tall when he died. It is conservatively estimated that had he lived to manhood he would have reached 6 feet.[25] In addition to this, his postcranial skeleton (that portion below the skull) was found to be so similar to that of modern man that Alan Walker, coleader of Leakey's team, said that an average pathologist could not tell them apart! Furthermore, when a jaw was placed on the skull, it looked remarkably like the Neanderthal Man, whose fossils have been classified as true man.

In spite of all this, the boy's fossils were classified a step below Neanderthal. Leakey placed these fossils within the classification known as *Homo erectus* (above Lucy, but below modern man). As was the case with Johanson, I believe that the supposed age of these fossils affected Leakey's decision.[26] After all, evolutionists maintain that Neanderthal didn't evolve until anywhere from 300 thousand to 100 thousand years ago.[27] Since this boy is supposedly much older than that, Leakey probably felt forced to classify him in a more primitive category, even if he had to ignore the physical evidence in order to do so.

According to Leakey, this boy's fossils are 1.6 million years old, yet they are so similar to modern men that even a pathologist would have difficulty distinguishing the two. Remember also that this boy was well on his way to being 6 feet tall and looked at least as good as Neanderthal, who in turn looked like the gentleman in the gray flannel suit whom you may have seen in the mall last week. We can now begin to see the problem which these recent discoveries have presented to the evolutionists. *Using Leakey's dates they are forced to admit that only 200 thousand years separated Johanson's 3-feet-tall primate, which lived 1.8 million years ago, and Leakey's unquestionably human boy, who lived 1.6 million years ago.*

The evolutionists are now faced with the task of convincing both themselves and us that in only 200 thousand years (which is really no more than a drop in the evolutionists' time bucket) all of the following changes took place:

1. We increased in size from 3 feet to 6 feet.
2. Our long arms shortened.
3. Our curved fingers both shortened and straightened out.
4. Our curved toes also became shorter and straighter.
5. Our brain size doubled.

6. Our primitive skeletons took on totally modern features.

They try to tell us that these changes occurred in less than 200 thousand years in spite of the fact that Johanson's primates retained their long arms, long curved fingers and toes, and small brains for 2 million years (the time span between *Australopithecus afarensis* and *Homo habilis*).

Even though Johanson's primates supposedly remained under 3.5 feet tall for 2 million years, we are now supposed to believe that we evolved to 6 feet in just 200 thousand years. Even though Johanson's primate's brain remained unchanged for 2 million years, we are supposed to now believe that in 200 thousand years the brain evolved to double its previous size. What's even more astounding is that they are also trying to tell us that in the past 1.6 million years there have been comparatively few changes in the human line. Remember, one of their own admitted that the skeleton of Leakey's new find is virtually indistinguishable from that of men today.

The evolutionists' own words and calculations have now forced them to take the position that there were 2 million years of no change between Johanson's two finds. This period was in turn followed by a span of 200 thousand years in which massive changes occurred (the supposed time span between the lifetime of Johanson's latest find and that of Leakey's). These two periods were themselves followed by 1.6 million years of virtually no change within the human lineage (the period from the time when Leakey's discovery lived until now). It seems clear then that Johanson's and Leakey's discoveries do not support the theory of evolution—punctuated or otherwise.

What they do support is the fact that when man appeared on the earth, he was fully formed and was virtually indistinguishable from modern man. What they further reveal is that while man and the primates share certain anatomical features, they were, are now, and always will be distinctly separate creatures. Once again, the evolutionists made exaggerated claims which later discoveries have totally invalidated. Some prominent evolutionists however are now willing to admit that in reality the "tremendous amount of well-publicized information about the human fossil record" may in fact be well publicized, but it proves absolutely nothing. Sir Solly Zuckerman, himself a confirmed evolutionist, acknowledges that as to "the interpretation of man's fossil history, where to the faithful [evolutionist] anything is possible...the ardent believer is sometimes able to believe several contradictory things at the same time...[If man] evolved from some ape-like creature...[it was] *without leaving any fossil traces of the steps of the transformation.* "[28]

Seemingly undaunted by all this, the evolutionists charge ahead. They have been quick to claim that the extinct archaeoperyx was an intermediate between the reptiles and the birds. Archaeopteryx fossils have been found in the Upper Jurassic limestone formations of Bavaria. According to the evolutionists' dating methods, this makes them 150 million years old. While the archaeopteryx had fully developed feathers (and is therefore classified as a bird), it didn't have hollow bones or a keeled sternum. According to Eldredge, the "keeled sternum necessary for truly vigorous flight had not developed in the avian lineage."[29] In fact, he is so sure that it is an intermediary which cannot be explained away by the creationists that he states, "Bluster as they might, creationists cannot wriggle out of Archaeopteryx."[30]

Allow me the opportunity to "bluster" for a moment. If the fossil remains of a more "advanced" bird which appeared to be "older" than archaeopteryx were to be found, it would be the evolutionist and not the creationist who would be on the horns of a dilemma. What if the fossils of a bird with more "modern" birdlike features, such as hollow bones and a keeled sternum, were to be found, and these were found in the Dockum formation which evolutionists maintain is 75 million years older than the Upper Jurassic? The evolutionists would then have to explain how the archaeopteryx "evolved" to have more "primitive" features than its supposed ancestor. How could archaeopteryx be a *transition* between reptile and bird when one of its supposed ancestors had more birdlike features than it did? Finally, how could the newly discovered fossils be considered a transition when the number of supposedly reptilian features it had were less than those of archaeopteryx which already classified as a true bird?

Apparently it is the evolutionist who must now "bluster" because such fossils have been found—several of them in fact.[31] The evolutionists who refused to accept archaeopteryx for what it apparently was, namely, a totally distinct, separate species of true bird, have now been forced to abandon the "fact" that it was a transition between reptile and bird.

However, as before, the damage has already been done, because at least one more generation of impressionable school children has been assured that evolution is as real as gravity.[32] The evidence upon which that assertion was based has, as it was so many times before, been proven false. As the knowledge of these new discoveries slowly filters down through the educational system, all the talk of archaeopteryx as a "transition" will go the way of the Neanderthal hunchback pictures. It will be quietly forgotten by the same evolutionistic "scientists" who previously assured us it was a *fact*. The only fact that remains is that if the archaeopteryx fossils are indeed genuine they represent a separate, distinct species of true bird, and there still are no transition fossils between species.

The fossil record also fails to support the theory of evolution in regard to the fish, the amphibians, the mammals, and the plants. As we shall now see, there are at least some evolutionists who are willing to admit this is indeed the case. Concerning the plants, Chester A. Arnold, professor of biology and curator of fossil plants at the University of Michigan has stated that "[a]s of yet, we have *not been able to trace the phylogenetic history of a single group of modern plants from its beginning to the present.* "[33]

As for the fishes, J.R. Norman of the department of zoology at the British Museum of Natural History observed that "[t]he geological record has so far provided *no evidence as to the origin of the fishes.*"[34] Moving from fishes to amphibians, we find this disclosure by Barbara J. Stahl of St. Anselm's College, "...the *fossil material provides no evidence* of other aspects of the *transformation from fish to tetrapod,* [so] paleontologists have *had to speculate how legs and aerial breathing evolved...* ."[35] The supposed transition from reptile to mammal fares no better in the fossil record either.

Noted evolutionistic writer Roger Lewin has acknowledged the reptile/mammal connection to be nothing more than "an enigma."[36] At the same time, A.J. Kelso, professor of physical anthropology at the University of Colorado, accurately points out the fact that "*the transition from insectivore to primate is not documented by fossils.*"[37]

It is hard enough to believe scientists who are so easily taken in because of their intense desire to obtain proof for their theory, but the problem is compounded by what can only be described as a tendency on their part to mislead the general public when it comes to the supposed evidence of Darwinian evolution. Whether this tendency is intentional or simply the result of carelessness, I will not presume to judge. I leave that to the reader.

A prime example of this tendency can be seen in the fossil remains of what has become known as Java Man. Those fossil remains, which have been termed an intermediate between modern man and his apelike ancestors, consisted of a skullcap and a thighbone. They were discovered by Eugene Dubois who noted that the skullcap was apelike in appearance, but the thighbone was without a doubt that of a modern man. It was not made known until 30 years after Dubois reported his discovery that some normal, modern-man skullcaps also were present in the same area. Regardless of what fossils have or have not been found in other locations, the unanswered question is why did Dubois actively conceal the presence of modern-man skull bones within the same general formation when such information would have been paramount to any impartial evaluation of his find?

It is more important that this further question be answered, Why has the evolutionistic community continued to acknowledge Dubois' fossils as an example of a transitional man when near the end of his life Dubois admitted that the skull he used for his "man" was in fact that of a giant gibbon?[38] The same mind-set which caused early evolutionists to continue accepting spontaneous generation as a viable explanation for the "origin" of life two hundred years after it had been disproved by William Harvey has caused the current crop of evolutionists to continue misrepresenting the fossil record to us.[39]

Before we continue discussion of the evolutionists' misrepresentation of the fossil record, allow me to point out that their tendency to create entire beings from as little evidence as one fossilized bone extends to the dinosaurs as well. According to *A Field Guide to Dinosaurs*, the *Arctosaurus* was developed from a single vertebra which previously had been thought to be that of a turtle. The *Diplotomodon*, the *Paronychodon*, and the *Macrodontophion* all were developed from single teeth. Furthermore, the single jaw used to develop the *Colonosaurus* could just as easily have belonged to a bird or sea lizard, while the four teeth used to construct the *Chienkosaurus* could just as likely have come from an ancient crocodile.[40]

While we are on this topic, it should probably be noted that the evolutionists' tendency to play fast and loose with fossil remains likewise extends to the dinosaurs. Many of us remember the pictures of the *Brontosaurus* dinosaur as featured in *B.C.* and *The Flintstones* cartoon strips. This denizen of the past with its huge body and small, slender head was also featured in numerous advertising campaigns. In fact, we have seen so many pictures of this creature that for many of us it is his image which comes to mind whenever we hear the word *dinosaur*. But there is a problem with that image. The brontosaur *as pictured* never existed. You see, the men who found the *Brontosaurus* fossils forgot to tell us that the skeleton they found was complete except for its head. This did not deter them though. What they did was take a skull which had been found about three miles away and put it on their skeleton, thereby creating the brontosaur. It has since been acknowledged that the brontosaur actually was composed of the skeleton of a diplodocus and the skull of an apatosaur.[41] If *errors* of this type have been made when whole skeletons have been found, how can we blindly accept the notion that there were as many different species of dinosaurs as these men assure us there were? This is especially so when we remember that many of their creations are based upon only one or two fossils.

But there is an even more compelling reason to be skeptical of any evolutionist's interpretation of the fossil record. Allow me to point out that between 1940 and 1980 the entire evolutionistic community was hiding the fact that the fossil record simply did not support the theory of gradual transitions between major groups. While one evolutionist has said it is a "vicious lie" for creationists to accuse his colleagues of such unprofessional actions, as we saw earlier, his own colleague made the very same accusation.[42] This colleague even went so far as to state that the active conspiracy to hide the lack of transitional evidence from the general public has

been the *"trade secret"* of the paleontologist.[43] I am therefore forced to ask this question, Why should we believe any
supposed "science" which keeps as a "trade secret" the very
facts which Darwin himself said would destroy his theory?

In some instances evolutionists have even made conflicting statements themselves. Eldredge said in his book *Monkey Business* (page 98) that creationists were not accurate in
accusing his colleagues of ignoring the very fossil evidence
which disproves Darwin's theory of gradual evolution. However, in his other book, *Time Frames* (pages 187-189), he
makes the very same accusation himself. Therein he states
that "the old paleontological reaction...was to throw out
genetics or invent a seemingly more suitable...theory... .
[N]early every paleontologist who reviewed Darwin's
Origin of the Species pointed to his [Darwin's] *evasion* of
this salient feature of the fossil record." It should be noted
that the salient feature of the fossil record which Darwin
evaded was the fact that there is no evidence within it to support his notion of gradual transitions.

Don't think for one minute that Darwin was not acutely
aware of what he was doing. In order for Darwin to establish
the plausibility of the very idea of evolution "Darwin felt that
he had to *undermine* the older—doctrine of species fixity."[44]
This was not going to be easy because the fossil record simply did not support Darwin's theory. What the fossil record
does show us is that (using Eldredge's own words) "all the
different species tend to remain remarkably stable, recognizable entities for millions of years."[45] While I strongly disagree with Eldredge's assessment concerning the time frame

involved, I do most certainly agree that species do remain remarkably stable.

It was this very fact of species stability which remained (again using Eldredge's own words) an "ugly inconvenience" for Darwin. Therefore, Darwin simply ignored it.[46] Not only did Darwin intentionally sidestep this issue, but Eldredge points out that "stasis [Eldredge's own word for species stability] had continued to be ignored until Gould and I showed that such stability...must be confronted."[47] But even they did not confront the issue of species stability until 1972. This means that evolutionists for 115 years had been ignoring the very facts which Darwin himself knew disproved his entire theory of gradual evolution. What's just as interesting is that even when Eldredge and Gould attempted to confront this issue, all they could offer us was "punctuated equilibria." As we have already seen, Eldredge admits that as late as 1985, 12 years after it was initially proposed, this notion was still not yet totally thought through or completely testable!

The evolutionist therefore still is faced with the same problem we first saw in Chapter 2. The facts clearly do not support the theory of evolution—punctuated or otherwise. Rather than acknowledge the only logical alternative (special creation), the evolutionist now must hold on to the totally unscientific notion called punctuated equilibria. Again, you do not need to rely solely upon my word for this. Robert E. Ricklefs, a professor of evolutionary biology at the University of Pennsylvania has been quoted as saying, "The punctuated equilibrium model has been widely accepted, not because it has a compelling theoretical basis, *but because it appears to resolve a dilemma.*" The dilemma of course is that the fossil record simply does not support Darwin's theory. Ricklefs continued his observation by noting that the punctuated equilibria "model is *more* ad hoc *explanation than theory, and it rests on shaky ground.*"[48]

As you may recall, Eldredge, in his book *Monkey Business,* (page 130) explained the lack of Precambrian intermediate fossils by stating that since these supposed intermediates were "soft bodied," it was "extremely unlikely" that they would have become fossilized. Yet, in the very same book (page 44) he acknowledges the existence of numerous fossilized "soft bodied creatures…[including those] of the—jellyfish phylum…up to seven feet long…[from places] as far flung as Australia, Newfoundland, England, Siberia, and South Africa." Needless to say, conflicting statements of this type only lead to more confusion.

Why should we now believe any group of scientists who insist that "students ought to know that the evidence for evolution has been scrupulously scrutinized daily by thousands of biologists for well over a hundred years…,"[49] when the scrupulous scrutinizers we are expected to wholeheartedly believe have either purposely withheld the "trade secret" that graduated transitional evidence does not exist or were not observant enough to notice the obvious? If indeed a thousand such biologists spent only two hours per working day for one hundred years scrutinizing this evidence, we would have 26 million man hours of research which was either devoted to a cover up or was so incompetent that it could not even see that what it was looking for obviously did not exist.

In either case, it really doesn't matter. You could have 1 billion hours of the type of scrutinization which failed to notice the *hoax* of Piltdown Man, the *mistake* of Nebraska Man, the *oversight* of Neanderthal Man's rickets, or the *rush to judgment* represented by the belief that *Archaeopteryx* was a transition, and it would still not make the evidence for evolution any more valid or scientific. This type of scrutinization merely compounds the wishful thinking of those early evolutionists which led to the eloquently fabricated assertions as to why the known facts did not conform to what the evolutionists *knew* was true.

Eldredge states that while there is dissent within the ranks of evolutionists today, "...as recently as a decade ago there was something approaching unanimity" among his colleagues. I submit to you that this unanimity was the direct result of the decision by the vast majority of his colleagues to make up what he himself referred to as "eloquent" stories explaining why the fossil record did not support something which their preconceived notions told them it had to support. Further, I submit that the dissension which appears within the ranks of the evolutionists today is not the result of "willing admissions by paleontologists [who are evolutionists] concerned with accuracy," as some would have us believe, but that it is the direct result of true scientists being no longer willing to put up with the travesty to impartial research which such "trade secrets" represent.[50]

Concerning the willingness of evolutionary paleontologists to admit their errors, it should be noted that Henry Fairfield Osborn, who was the driving force behind the

Nebraska Man fiasco, never publicly acknowledged his gross error in assigning a pig molar to a high primate. In spite of the fact that it was his own expedition which inadvertently turned up the evidence which sounded the death knoll for Nebraska Man, Osborn himself refused to openly recognize the facts. Instead, all he did was conveniently fail ever again to mention the Nebraska Man in any of his subsequent writings on man's supposedly evolutionary ancestry.[51] But then he is not alone. Stephen Jay Gould admits that if you have read any evolutionary material produced in the past 50 years, "...you will probably not have encountered Hesperopithecus... ."[52]

Another example of the confusing statements which are made by evolutionists concerns the issue of brain size in man's supposed ancestors. According to M.F. Ashley Montagu in *An Introduction to Physical Anthropology*[53] and Carleton S. Coon in *The Story of Man*[54]—the very textbook I used in an undergraduate anthropology course, the brain size of the average Neanderthal Man was one hundred cubic centimeters *larger* than that of the average person today. The 1965 edition of the *Encyclopedia Britannica*[55] reports the finding that the average brain capacity of Cro-Magnon Man was at least two hundred cubic centimeters *larger* than that of modern man.

Why would any evolutionist then state, "Our own lineage shows progressive increase in both absolute body size and relative brain size...brain size has increased within our lineage"?[56] Since modern men have smaller brains, but are physically larger than our supposed ancestors, there is a definite discrepancy between his statement and the purportedly measurable facts. Or are we to believe that man's brain evolved by first getting bigger and then smaller? On the other hand, if Neanderthal Man and Cro-Magnon Man, both of whom had larger brains than modern men, are not part of our heritage, why are they always included in the evolutionists' charts?[57]

If the measurements are wrong, then the evolutionists are extremely careless and should therefore not be taken seriously when they toss around figures such as 4 billion years. If the measurements are correct, then why would the statement have been made? Perhaps it is an attempt to tell us that "relative brain size" means that while modern man's brain is physically smaller than that of his ancestors, we can somehow tell that portions of it were obviously larger or more useful. But that is nothing more than pure speculation, nothing more than hazarding a guess.[58] That would not be the statement of a scientist who makes statements based solely upon observation. After all, there are no fossilized brains available for examination.

Even other evolutionists have recognized that to say one can determine the function of a brain by measuring its size is "extremely dangerous." To say that you can determine the function of a brain by measuring the skull is "extremely difficult, if not impossible." Why? Because about the "all important internal circuitry [of early man's brain] we know nothing."[59] As to which is in error—the statement or the measurements, I do not know. Either one casts a shadow of doubt over the "scientific" nature of the theory of evolution.

However, fluctuating sizes is not the only problem facing evolutionists when the topic of the human brain is raised.

Even though atheistic evolutionists such as Isaac Asimov will acknowledge that the human brain" is the most complex and orderly arrangement of matter in the universe," they still insist that we accept their notion that this most miraculous organ evolved by mere chance.[60]

Exactly how complex is the brain? I'm glad you asked. The average human brain contains about 10 billion neurons. Each neuron is in contact with as many as 10 thousand other neurons by means of connections called dendrites. The total number of neuron interconnections is approximately 1 thousand trillion. Just how many connections is that? Again, I'm glad you asked. According to the evolutionist Michael Denton, a fair analogy would be as follows:

> Imagine an area about half the size of the USA (one million square miles) covered in a forest...containing ten thousand trees per square mile. If each tree contained ten thousand leaves, the total number of leaves in the forest would be...equivalent to the number of connections in the human brain.[61]

As inconceivable as it may be when we consider this information, most evolutionists still expect us to accept their notion that the brain evolved by chance, either as a result of natural selection[62] or by mutation.[63] What is even more inconceivable is that these claims are made in spite of the fact that many other evolutionists, such as Jeffrey S. Wicken of the biochemistry department at Behrend College, have finally acknowledged that "*random mutation is inadequate* both in scope and theoretical grounding" to serve as the mechanism by which such an organ could have come into existence.[64] While natural selection does indeed produce changes *within* species, such prominent evolutionists as Steven M. Stanley of the department of earth and planetary sciences at John Hopkins University also concede that "[g]radual evolutionary change by natural selection operates so slowly within established species that it *cannot account for the major features of evolution.*"[65]

Needless to say, not only have the "waters" of the theory of evolution been troubled by "trade secrets," hoaxes, horrendous oversights, poor judgment, and flawed research, but now they have been hopelessly poisoned by the continued acceptance of disproven and discounted propositions such as natural selection and mutation.

Chapter 5

Let's Assume

Niles Eldredge's statements are used to "make a forceful fascinating case for the continuous teaching of evolution" in our public schools.[1] However, he is the "scientist" who cites the authority of a reader survey in *Glamour* magazine to establish the point that creationist thinking has been gaining ground in America. I am not discrediting *Glamour* magazine, but I am sure that the Gallup poll uses a much more scientific approach to polling than does *Glamour*, but then *Glamour* makes no pretense of being scientific—evolutionists do.

Scientists should not rely upon reader surveys in *Glamour* magazine nor circular reasoning to establish their points, but evolutionists have been known to do both. Eldredge maintains that the accusation that his geologist colleagues use or have used circular reasoning is "serious...and...of course, false."[2] His denial though needs to be evaluated in light of David M. Raup's admission that "[t]he charge that the construction of the geologic scale involves circularity has a certain amount of validity."[3] (If you will recall, David Raup is chairman of the geophysical sciences department of the University of Chicago.)

The use of circular reasoning also needs to be evaluated in light of admissions by other evolutionists who concede the obvious. In 1956 R.H. Rastall, writing for *Encyclopedia Britannica*, observed that "from a strictly philosophical standpoint geologists are...arguing in a circle."[4] Twenty years later J.E. O'Rourke not only reaffirmed the point that "circularity is inherent to the derivation of time scales," but added that "geologist[s]...[have] never bothered to think of a good reply [to the charge of circularity] feeling that explanations are not worth the trouble as long as the work brings results."[5] In other words, even though the circular reasoning processes upon which evolutionists have relied leaves much to be desired from the intellectual standpoint, they have never felt compelled to justify their position, because too many gullible people have been willing to accept what they said at face value.

Concerning the whole issue of fossil age, you might well ask "How did evolutionists arrive at the dates of fossils?" Their answer would be "From the position fossils occupy in the rock in which they are found, the oldest being on the bottom, the youngest on top." That seems to make sense. However, if you inquire as to how they arrive at the dates for the rocks themselves, you might be told, "By observing what fossils are found in them." You see, evolutionists *know* that the fossils found in Cambrian rock formations must be hundreds of millions of years old. Therefore, the rocks in which they are found must also be of the same age. "Hold it," you exclaim, "that's not scientific!" Maybe not, but it worked for them for over a hundred years until they latched on to radioisotope dating techniques.

Isotope dating is critical to the theory of evolution because it results in dates which seem to help the evolutionists overcome the horrendous mathematical improbabilities presented by their theory. Notice that I said "seems to help" them. In reality, even the dates determined by isotope dating are not old enough to bring the theory of evolution into the realm of mathematical possibilities. At first evolutionists thought carbon-14 dating would give them the hundreds of millions of years they needed. It did not, so it was discarded as unreliable for anything more than a few thousand years old.[6]

Isotope dating is based upon man's ability to accurately measure the rate of decomposition of a material from one form into another. The rock itself cannot be dated, only the material which is found in it. *If* we know how much of the original (parent) material was in the rock when the rock was formed, and *if* we know how much of the subsequent (daughter) material was also in the rock when the rock was formed, and *if* we assume the rate of decay from parent into daughter has been constant for the past billion or so years, and finally, *if* we assume that nothing has acted upon either the parent or daughter material in such a way so as to alter the amount of either material present during this entire billion-year period, *then* we can measure the amount of the parent material still in the rock, the amount of daughter material still in the rock, apply the rate of decay, and thereby estimate the age of the rock. *Phew*, those are a lot of assumptions.

Since it is impossible to test the assumption that the rate of decay determined today has been the same for several billion years, all I can say is that it takes a great deal of "faith" to believe it. However, several points need to be considered before the other assumptions can be accepted. In isotope dating two separate materials are involved in the dating process; the parent and the daughter. Various elements found in *common groundwater* have been found to dissolve virtually every one of the parent elements and the subsequent daughter elements into which they decompose. What's more, this dissolving process can be faster in the parent than it is in the daughter and vice versa. Needless to say, this could and would drastically affect the age derived from any dating process which must assume that both the parent and daughter elements have *never* been affected by any other agent during their supposed 4-billion-year history. Since many, if not all, of these elements could have been exposed to such agents during the Genesis flood, I do not feel that I can accept either the assumption that no agent ever affected these elements or that we can accurately know the original amount of either the parent or daughter element present in the rock when the rock was formed.

In spite of the fact that most evolutionists leave the impression that isotope dating is foolproof, some of them have been willing to admit that everything is not quite as settled as they would have us believe. Frederic B. Jueneman has acknowledged that "[t]here has been in recent years the horrible realization that radiodecay rates are not as constant as previously thought, nor are they immune to environmental influences."[7]

Furthermore, by definition Darwinian evolution assumes that all things started out at age zero and then got older. If an evolutionist had been invited to the wedding at Cana, he would have been able to *prove* to his own satisfaction that the wine served at the end of the wedding banquet was the oldest because it had a finer bouquet and more body than the wine served earlier (see John 2:1-11). Even though, as Robert Jastrow informed us, true scientists have discovered that the world had a beginning under conditions in which the known laws of physics did not apply, evolutionistic scientists must of necessity deny the existence of a Creator God who used forces supposedly no longer at work today. Thus, there is no possibility that the evolutionist could accept the "story" that one of the wedding guests had anything to do with the "creation" of this fine beverage, even if His name was Jesus. After all, the evolutionist could tell by his five senses that this wine was more than just a few minutes old. Therein lies the problem.

Any evolutionist would feel duty bound to find a purely naturalistic explanation for this wine's existence. In the natural realm wine comes from fermented grape juice. Needless to say, for good wine this process takes a minimum of several months. Therefore, since the evolutionist is compelled by his beliefs to deny God, he would ignore the fact that the jugs in question had been filled with water only moments before the wine appeared. But then that is exactly what evolutionists have been doing since Darwin first proposed his theory. They conveniently overlook facts which they themselves have observed, when those facts interfere with their naturalistic explanations. The evolutionists' prejudice against God is stronger than their desire to find the truth. In short, the problem is not their search for naturalistic explanations which account for the phenomena we observe in the physical world; that after all is what science does. The problem is that evolutionists insist upon naturalistic explanations for *all* occurrences, even when those explanations cause them to ignore either the observable facts or the very laws of science which serve as the basis for all scientific inquiry.

An intellectually honest, truth-seeking scientist will acknowledge all the facts with which he is faced. When no naturalistic explanation can be postulated which both accounts for these facts and complies with the known laws of nature, he will admit that the occurrence he is investigating cannot be adequately explained by modern science. The occurrence being studied may in fact be supernatural in origin. If it were, then no naturalistic explanation would be correct, no matter how well thought through. The theory of evolution loses on both counts. First of all, it is incorrect, and secondly, it is not very well thought through.

The evolutionists' absolute prejudice against any supernatural occurrence causes them no end of difficulties. For example, they deny the possibility that any star could have been created with its path of light to earth already established. They assume that since some particular star is a million light years away and we can see it now, then that star must have been in existence for a million light years, otherwise we couldn't see its light. Let me emphasize that there is no empirical evidence to support such a conclusion. As noted by astrogeophysicist Dr. John A. Eddy, a solar astronomer at the High Altitude Observatory at Boulder, Colorado, "There is *no evidence based solely on solar observation* that the sun is 4.5-5 x 10^9 years old." As an evolutionist he admits that all he can do is *"suspect* that the sun is 4.5 billion years old."[8] However, this insistence upon the antiquity of the universe, which the evolutionists have calculated by means of their naturalistic reasoning methods, works against them just as it did in the area of geologic uniformitarianism.

If evolutionists combine this concept of the age of the universe with the projected life expectancy of the sun, they are faced with a real problem. According to astronomers, the universe is expanding. That is to say, the distance between each individual star is actually increasing. However, should this process continue at its present rate for a period of time equal to only one-fifth of the estimated remaining life expectancy of our sun, the night sky would be void of stars when one looked up. Why? The distance between each star would have become so great that one would be unable to see them. The Big Dipper would disappear along with Orion the Hunter and all the other constellations. This of course puts the evolutionist in direct conflict with the Scripture, which tells us that God created the stars in order to give us light at night (Gen. 1:17).

While evolutionists could care less about the Bible, they apparently don't like the idea of a dark night sky either. Thus, they have made a slight alteration in their uniformitarian thinking. Some of them will now tell you that obviously the universe must have gone through several periods of both expansion and contraction. In one instance the evolutionist rejects biblical creation because it requires a *miracle* and in the next instance he offers an idea such as the expansion and contraction of the entire universe and then expects us to believe that his idea is *natural*!

Some evolutionists have even gone so far as to use this same reasoning process to explain away the problem presented by the current level of the ocean's salinity (noted earlier). It has been postulated that given the present rate at which salt is being added to the oceans and their present level of salinity, they could not possibly be more than a few hundred thousand years old. Since the evolutionists *know* that the world is at least 4 billion years old, they have come up with an explanation for the present level of ocean salinity. Since necessity is the mother of invention, the theory of salt cycles was developed. What must have happened, according to this theory, is that the oceans have gone through several periods wherein salt has alternately been added to and subtracted from the oceans. By some unknown process salt passed from the oceans back into the continental rock structure and then back into the oceans. Needless to say, it is maintained that this happened in such a way that this highly corrosive, readily soluble, migratory compound did not adversely affect the elements which are used for isotope dating. It is from these that evolutionists derived the huge numbers which created the necessity for the salt-cycle theory in the first place! Such reasoning reminds me of a children's nursery rhyme we all know quite well, "Here we go 'round the mulberry bush." I find it interesting that such theories can be taken seriously by anyone who can in one breath deny that a God has worked in the past using processes supposedly no longer observable today and then "exhale" an hypothesis which indicates that this is exactly what his "science" is doing.

Creationists who accept the biblical account of the great flood are considered religious zealots in spite of the vast quantity of geologic evidence which supports this event.[9] While even though no evidence exists to support their notions, evolutionists who propose totally untestable hypotheses which require an expanding and contracting universe and oceanic salt cycles are considered scientific.

There is still one other hypothesis that evolutionists have proposed which requires more faith than Noah's ark ever did. Evolutionists have conceded that the fossil record supports the fact that at least 90 percent of all species of animals, including dinosaurs, suffered mass extinction.[10] In fact, many evolutionists now believe that there were as many as 12 mass extinctions, with five of them being global in scope.[11] Since they refuse to accept the idea that the geologic layers which contain the evidence for those extinctions were virtually all laid down as the result of the biblical great flood, evolutionists must of necessity invent separate causes for the fossils which appear in each of the several distinct layers. How do evolutionists account for the largest of these episodes of mass extinction? Combining the best elements of science fiction with all the power of a disaster movie, the "science" which first proposed salt cycles now unveils "the giant asteriod."

This hypothesis, first presented by Luis and Walter Alvarez, goes something like this: A giant asteriod struck the earth, sending a huge cloud of dust and gas into the air. This cloud was so thick that it literally blocked out the sun throughout the entire world for several months. Without adequate sunlight, photosynthesis stopped, thereby killing all the plants. Due to the loss of their food sources, those dinosaurs which ate plants died. Along with them, the meat-eating dinosaurs, who consumed the plant-eating ones, also disappeared. When the dust settled and sunlight returned, new plants sprang up from the seeds in the soil. Any dinosaurs which had somehow managed to survive this process were killed off by the ice age which followed on the heels of the sun-blocking dust cloud which in addition to killing off the plants had cooled the earth's surface.

Since no crater can be found anywhere on or below the earth's surface to point to an impact of this magnitude, it has been conveniently assumed that this asteriod must have landed in the ocean. But this by no means solves the evolutionists' problems. According to Edward Anders, a cosmochemist at the University of Chicago, "Even if it hit in the ocean, the impact would have created a crater 300 kilometers across… ."[12] Why so large? Even as Alvarez admits, in order for an asteriod to have done that much damage, it must have been at least ten kilometers (six miles) across.[13] What's more, it would have had to travel through space at 60 times the speed of sound and then hit the earth with 10 thousand times more power than any of the world's nuclear weapons.[14]

The biggest crater which can be found anywhere on or under the earth is only 32 kilometers across. Most scientists admit, though, this is no where near large enough to account for even one single episode of mass extinction.[15] Evolutionists who will not accept the Genesis flood as the explanation for the mass extinction which they themselves observed to have taken place are now faced with a most interesting paradox. They have no trouble finding the fossils of six-inch-long trilobites which were supposedly killed by Alvarez's asteriod, but they can't seem to find the 180-mile-wide crater such an impact must have created.

Furthermore, this far-fetched hypothesis totally fails to explain *how* dinosaurs and vegetation became buried under hundreds or even thousands of feet of *sedimentary* rock, thereby enabling these materials to become fossilized. (Remember, things which die and lie on the surface or are buried under a few inches of dust decompose, they do not become fossils.) If proponents of this theory hold to the position that this asteriod impact created a worldwide flood, they should be reminded that the Genesis account of the flood contains more verifiable data than does their "it came from outer space" theory.

In reality, what these evolutionists have done is base their entire hypothesis upon the fact that the level of iridium found on the earth is higher in some geologic layers than in others. While this is indeed true, it should be pointed out that the highest concentrations of this element are not located on the floors of any ocean, where this asteriod supposedly hit, but in South Africa, Brazil, and Tasmania.

Furthermore, to argue that only the impact of a giant asteriod could account for these higher levels of iridium is ridiculous. It would make as much sense for me to say that the higher levels of nickel found in some areas of the earth resulted from a collision with the moon simply because the surface of the moon contains a higher level of nickel than is normally found in earth. After all, there is as much geologic evidence to support my notion as there is for Alvarez's giant asteriod story. However, I acknowledge that my hypothesis is not scientific; whereas the evolutionists, by including the asteriod idea as part of their theory, insist that Alvarez's notion be treated as scientific.

The evolutionists have again offered a totally untestable hypothesis as part of their science and in the process have again violated the first rule of true science. Knowingly or unknowingly, they have again called God a liar. If in fact an asteriod-induced "nuclear winter" did occur and lasted several years, then God has not only lied to us, but He even lied to Himself. You see, Genesis 8:21-22 tells us that after the flood God "said in His heart…[a]s long as the earth endures, seedtime and harvest, cold and heat, summer and winter, day and night will never cease." This of course does not mean that there will not be local disasters like flooding, drought, or even darkened skies following some volcanic eruptions, but God has specifically promised that these will not be worldwide.

There are numerous other problems presented by the theory of evolution and its fundamental premise that the lower progresses into the higher, but lack of space prevents me from discussing them. The highlights I have presented thus far however are sufficient to point out three things: First, evolution is in direct, irreconcilable conflict with the Bible. Neither the Bible nor pure evolutionistic thought allows one to take merely a portion of each and forget the rest. Second, by definition, totally evolutionistic thought denies the existence of a Creator God. Third, neither the account of the origin of life as found in Genesis nor that postulated by any form of evolutionary theory is scientific. Both are the account of the creation of the world and man, one from the viewpoint of Judeo/Christian religion and the other from the viewpoint of the religion called secular humanism.

From the outset of this study I have made clear what I believe. I accept creation as a *fact*. Even if we momentarily set aside all the physical evidence with clearly points to this event, I have the Bible to substantiate my position. Evolutionists accept evolution as a *fact*, and as you can see from what we have discussed so far, they have nothing more than controverted reasoning, misleading statements, faulty assumptions, and outright hoaxes to prove what they believe.

Before continuing any further, please allow me to clear up a misconception which is shared by many people. There is a vast difference between scientific creationism and the Genesis account of creation. The Genesis account of creation describes not only the origin of all things, but it tells us who the originator was. Since no one except God was around at the time, the human thought process which depends upon observation and reasoning cannot explain this event. Any discussion concerning the origin of the species is in fact totally beyond the limits of scientific inquiry. As Robert Jastrow has so aptly noted, the world had a beginning under conditions in which the known laws of physics are not valid. Origins are in fact supernatural.

On the other hand, those who adhere to scientific creationism by following established rules of procedure, observation, and experimentation analyze the physical evidence which is all around us today in an attempt to explain by what process things change and how both these processes and the organisms they affect interrelate. When the facts revealed by this process of examination clearly point toward an act of creation, the creation scientist is willing to admit that in all likelihood his investigation can go no further and still remain within the bounds of purely scientific inquiry.

The evolutionist however will either deny the very facts which his own investigation has uncovered, or he will misrepresent them. Therefore, he will continue moving backward in time until he has abandoned all pretext of scientific inquiry. At that point he will have left the world of true science and entered into the realm of science fiction—otherwise known as the "twilight zone"—wherein dwells Goldschmidt's "hopeful monster," Alvarez's "giant asteriod," and Crick's "intergalactic protein molecule."

While I have not touched upon all the scientific discoveries which clearly demonstrate a special creation, do not make the mistake of thinking that there aren't any. Up to this point in our discussion I have concentrated upon many of the shortcomings of the evolutionists' position. While this will continue to be my general thrust, I would like to highlight merely a few of these discoveries in order to alleviate any fears you may have that there are no truly scientific facts which substantiate the creationists' position. Again, let me reiterate that I am only going to highlight just a few of them. It would take several volumes to do justice to this topic alone, but that is not the intent of this book. Should you wish to delve deeper into the nature of these facts, I suggest that you check the bibliography which appears at the end of this volume. For now, here is a brief summary of five of those discoveries and the concepts which clearly point to a special creation:

1. *Principle of universal causation.* As acknowledged even by the evolutionist Abraham Wolf, former professor and chairman of the department of history and methods of science at the University of London, this principle shows us the following: One cause can have many effects; however, no effect can be quantitatively greater than or qualitatively superior to its cause.[16] When this principle is applied to the origins of the universe we discover the following:

   1. The first cause of limitless space must be infinite.
   2. The first cause of endless time must be eternal.
   3. The first cause of boundless energy must be omnipotent.
   4. The first cause of infinite complexity must be omniscient.
   5. The first cause of life must be living.

   Therefore the first cause of the universe must be infinite, eternal, omnipotent, omniscient, and living, which is exactly the position taken by creationists.

2. *First law of thermodynamics.* According to Isaac Asimov, perhaps the best-known advocate of the atheistic/humanistic/evolutionistic position, the first law of thermodynamics can be summarized as follows: "The total quantity of energy in the universe is constant." He continues his definition by noting that this law "is considered the most powerful and most fundamental generalization about the universe that scientists have ever been able to make.... [I]n over a century and a quarter of careful measurements scientists have never

been able to point to a definite violation of energy con-servation."[17] Using the evolutionists' own definition for this law we arrive at a most interesting conclusion. Since the quantity of energy has never been more or less than it is today, the universe must have come into existence with its level of energy already in place. This speaks not of gradual development, but of a moment of creation.

3. *Second law of thermodynamics.* To quote Asimov again, the second law of thermodynamics can be expressed as follows: "The universe is constantly getting more disor-derly."[18] From this fact we know that the amount of ener-gy *available for use* grows smaller with each passing day, even though the *quantity* of energy throughout the universe remains constant. Just as a watch spring which is half run down was once fully wound, so also must there have been a moment in the past when every bit of that quantity of universal energy was available for use. That moment was at its point of creation.

4. *Genetic code.* As you may recall from our earlier discus-sion, Louis Pasteur proved by experimentation that the very premise of spontaneous generation was false. Fur-thermore, if we assume that living matter is greater than nonliving matter, the principle of universal causation also falsifies this premise. Not only must evolutionists overcome these two problems, but recent discoveries concerning the genetic code have thrown a major mon-key wrench into their works. In fact, after being faced with proof that a genetic code of some type is found in all living organisms, even the confirmed evolutionist Leslie Orgel acknowledged in 1982 that "the origin of the genetic code is the most baffling aspect of the origins of

life."[19] The reason that the evolutionists have such difficulty with this code is the discovery that the genetic information which is found in an organism is itself specified by the genetic code of that organism's parents. In other words, *there is no other means by which it can be transmitted or received by the organism in which it is found other than by inheritance.*

Furthermore, Sir Fred Hoyle, the noted British evolutionistic astronomer calculated the odds which had to be overcome in order for the *first* self-reproducible protein to arise by chance from the primordial soup which evolutionists assume covered the earth billions of years ago. Those odds were 1 in 10 to the 40-thousandth power. That's 10 followed by 40 thousand zeros! Because of the mathematical impossibility of this taking place on earth by chance, Hoyle joined forces with Francis Crick in assuming that life must have evolved in some other portion of the universe where conditions were presumably more favorable and then traveled to earth by some unknown means.[23] The point is recent discoveries concerning the genetic code tell us that some type of code was in the first representative of each of the original species on the earth. Since it could only be placed there through inheritance, it must have been placed there by a living Creator.

5. *Predictability of scientific theory.* Every valid scientific theory must of necessity be able to suggest what some future researcher should discover as he continues his investigations. The theory of creation has been in existence longer than has the intellectual exercise we call science.

From its very beginnings however creation has made numerous predictions which have now been discovered to be completely accurate. The facts of the fossil record and the laws of mathematical probability which we have discussed in other sections of this book all have verified the following points:

1. The theory of creation suggested that distinct and complex organisms would appear in the fossil record without leaving any record of fossilized ancestors.

2. The theory of creation suggested that basic categories of plants and animals would be widely distributed even at the point where they first appeared in the fossil record.

3. The theory of creation suggested that living organisms are far too complex to be the mere product of random selection.

4. The theory of creation suggested that mutations and microevolutionary changes would be neutral, harmful, or degenerative in their effect.

To the truth-seeking, intellectually honest scientist, the discoveries we have looked at in this section are exactly what they purpose to be, namely, the results of scientific research which clearly points to a special creation. According to Robert Jastrow, however, facts such as these place the evolutionists in the middle of a "bad dream:" The evolutionist has "scaled the mountain of ignorance; he is about to conquer the highest peak; as he pulls himself over the final rock, he is greeted by a band of theologians who have been sitting there for centuries."[21]

However, since most evolutionists don't like either bad dreams or evangelical theologians they simply ignore the facts we have just examined. Rather than acknowledge their error, they willingly go back down the mountain of ignorance into the valley of the absurd. They have chosen instead to walk along the path of the preposterous, where they are joined by their hiking companions, Piltdown Man and Nebraska Man.

Chapter 6

Holy Hydrogen and Hitler

Why would seemingly intelligent people accept such a theory as evolution? Secular humanism absolutely requires that they do so. If the theory of evolution is correct, then man is slowly evolving into a better and higher state and is therefore not in need of a personal Savior to redeem him. Just in case you think that I may have misinterpreted the evolutionists' position on this issue, allow me to call your attention to Richard Leakey's comments concerning the source of aggression in mankind. "Any aggression we show is the product of our culture and environment, *not our nature*."[1] In fact, the entire premise of Leakey's book *The People of the Lake* is that the driving force which transformed apes into humans is the natural sense of goodness and cooperation which existed among man's supposed ancestors. He believes that this natural tendency to cooperate somehow caused our ancestors' brains to enlarge as they were forced to cope with the increasingly complex society such cooperation fostered.

Since humanistic evolutionists maintain that man has no original sin, they further take the position that "salvation based upon mere affirmation," in the redemptive sacrifice of Jesus Christ is in reality a destructive philosophy which diverts man's attention from his true source of power. They hold to the belief that instead of looking to God "reasonable minds look to other means for survival."[2] Sir Julian Huxley, founder of the American Humanist Association, spelled out in no uncertain terms just where it is that mankind must now look, when he said, "...man...is not under the control or guidance of any supernatural being...but has to rely on himself and his own powers."[3]

On the other hand, if the Bible is correct, then man is not evolving; rather he has in fact gone from a state of perfection to one of sin and degradation from which he cannot be rescued except by the blood of Jesus Christ. Satan has come to kill, steal, and destroy (Jn. 10:10). As we have so clearly seen up to this point, he has skillfully used the tools of his trade to get many people to believe his theory. I am aware that this is a rather forceful statement, but in reality the topic we are dealing with is that of life and death.

Let's put it this way. If you were an astronaut about to take a ride on a Saturn IV rocket, how would you feel if you overheard one of the scientists who designed a major component of that rocket tell his colleagues that the design for that part had not been completely tested or for that matter even thoroughly thought through? Do you think that you would still be willing to put your life in his hands? I believe the intelligent answer to that question has to be no! However, when you accept the theory of evolution you are taking a much more dangerous ride. In the process you are putting more than your physical life on the line. Whether you know it or not, you may very well be placing your soul in the hands of just such "scientists."

By stating in his book that "the gloves are off," Eldredge acknowledges that the battle line has been drawn between creationists and evolutionists.[4] Unfortunately, the evolutionists have been very successful up to this point in claiming victims. All you have to do is turn to the supplementary volume to the *Interpreter's Dictionary of the Bible*, (1976 hardbound edition, pages 792-793) to see the inroads that evolution has made into liberal theology. When the liberal theologian assumes that scientific knowledge has rendered belief in the miracle of creation intellectually irresponsible, he is in reality saying that science provides us with knowledge of the limits within which God will always operate. Such a theologian has inadvertently made a god of scientific knowledge. However, if in fact an Almighty God does exist, then miracles are generally possible at every moment.

Make no mistake about it, evolution is a religious belief. Of course most evolutionists would deny this, but let's take a closer look at what evolutionists have actually said.[5] Concerning the teaching of the Genesis account of creation in science classes (something which I am not advocating as long as evolution is not taught there) Eldredge says, "Students should not be asked to *believe*, but they *should* be taught those things, such as evolution, that scientists **think** are true of the natural universe" (bold emphasis added)[6] *Roget's College Thesaurus* says that a synonym for the word *believe* is the word *think*. *The American College Dictionary*, 1960 edition, includes in its definitions for the word *think*, the following: "To hold as an opinion: *believe*: suppose."

Since Eldredge maintains that his science is not a "belief system," why then does he use words which are interchangeable, such as *think* and *believe*?[7] Why not use the word *know*, i.e., "scientists *know* are true of the natural universe"? The reason of course is that no true scientist would claim to *know* the reason for the sudden appearance of the multicellular life forms which are found in Cambrian rock, much less the origins of the universe. (Remember, even Eldredge admits that the appearance of Cambrian life forms is a mystery to his brand of science.) Therefore, he is correct in saying that evolutionistic scientists can only talk about what they think (i.e., what they believe) about the natural universe, and belief requires faith. It takes more faith to accept the notion that the undeniable order and symmetry which exists throughout the entire universe is a matter of sheer chance than it does to believe that it came about through the direct action of the Most High God.

Psalm 14:1 tells us, "The fool says in his heart, 'There is no God.' " While evolutionists are deceived, I would not call them fools; they do have a god. To discover who their god is, we have to travel back in time about 3 thousand years. Ancient Greek philosophy developed its own theory for the origins of all creatures. Around 100 B.C., a Roman poet name Lucretius set portions of his theory, which he had borrowed from the Greeks, to rhyme and lyric in order to make it more presentable to the average person of his day. Lucretius was cited approvingly by professor Sir Gavin de-Beer in his biology textbook *Adaption*, in which he says, "Chance was exactly what Lucretius invoked...to explain living creatures."[8]

Professor deBeer is correct in noting that Lucretius "invoked" chance. To invoke is to "call on a divine being" (*American College Dictionary*, 1960), and it is their "divine being"—chance—that evolutionists call upon. Evolutionists would have us believe that Cecil Alexander's beautiful poem should read, "All things bright and beautiful, all things great and small, all things wise and wonderful, the lord *chance* made them all," instead of "the Lord God made them all." Over the centuries believers in the chance development of the universe and life as we know it have dressed up their notion in order to accommodate what they perceived as man's increasing sophistication. They no longer use poetry to express this belief in "lord chance," now they call it "evolutionistic science."

Harlow Shapley, professor emeritus of astronomy at Harvard University expressed his evolutionistic fervor in this manner,

> Formerly the origin of life was held to be a matter for the Deity to take care of…But no longer. We now *believe* that all of the score of kinds of atoms evolved naturally from hydrogen… . To me it [evolution] is a *religious* attitude to recognize the wonder of the whole natural world. Not only life…why not *revere* also amino acids and the simple proteins from which life emerges.[9]

Not only have evolutionists crossed the line from science to religion, but Professor Shapley totally ignored the admonition of Deuteronomy 4:19, which tells us, "…when you look up to the sky and see the sun, the moon and stars—all the heavenly array—do not be enticed into bowing down to them and worshiping things the Lord your God has apportioned to all the nations under heaven." As noted in the New Testament, "In the past God overlooked such ignorance, but now He commands all people everywhere to repent" (Acts 17:30). As I said earlier, this is a matter of life and death.

The evolutionists have replaced the God of creation with the "creation god," and it is for them that Romans 1:21-22,25 comes into clear focus,

> *For although they knew God, they neither glorified Him as God nor gave thanks to Him, but their thinking became futile and their foolish hearts were darkened. Although they claimed to be wise, they became fools... . They exchanged the truth of God for a lie, and worshiped and served created things rather than the Creator—who is forever praised.*

> Romans 1:21-22, 25

Evolutionists may tell you that evolution is not a religious belief, but to put it in Shakespearean terms, a rose by any other name is still a rose.

There are at least a few brave evolutionists out there who are sheepishly willing to admit the fact that "evolutionistic science" has all the makings of a religious movement. Anthropology professor Dr. Loren Eiseley noted that he and fellow evolutionists were

> ...left in the somewhat embarrassing position of having to *postulate theories of living origins which [they] could not demonstrate.* After having chided the theologian for his reliance on myth and miracle, science found itself in the unenviable position of having

to *create a mythology of its own*; namely, the assumption that what, after long effort, could not be proved to take place had, in truth, taken place in the primeval past.[10]

Publicly however most evolutionists hold to the position that belief in a God who created all things requires an illogical leap of faith, whereas, according to them, salt cycles, giant asteroids, and an expanding and contracting universe constitute scientific principles which have nothing to do with faith. They have assured us that theirs is not a religious belief system, when in reality they cling to their beliefs as tenaciously as any cult member ever has. Instead of humbling themselves before the altar of repentance, they stand proudly before the altar of human reason. They have exchanged the supernatural Lord of the universe for the more "natural" universal law of chance. They have traded the miraculous account of life's inception for a more "naturalistic" although now thoroughly discounted concept called spontaneous generation. They put their faith not in Jesus Christ, the Rock of our salvation, but in the rocks of the geologic column. They have substituted the god of me, myself, and I for the one true God—Father, Son, and Holy Spirit. They have abandoned the Apostles' Creed, instead favoring the *Humanist Manifestos I and II*. Finally they have guided their lives not by the absolute standards of God's Word, but by the self-contradictory standard which assures us that there are absolutely no absolutes.

In an unsuccessful attempt to place as much distance as possible between the whole issue of religious morals and the theory of evolution, some evolutionists state that they cannot even begin to comprehend "[how] the ethical fabric of human social behavior is dependent upon one scenario or another about how we humans got here in the first place."[1] In one very limited sense they may be right, but not for the reasons they think. The philosophy of evolutionistic humanism is in fact devoid of morals and ethics, not because there is no relationship between the *topic* of evolution and the *topic* of ethics, but because the philosophical foundations of evolution are totally incapable of supporting any system of moral values. Before examining some very concrete examples of evolution's direct relationship to such things as genocide and racism, allow me to point out the predicament which evolutionistic humanists have created for themselves. I believe that you will see why it is that their philosophy leads to a total absence of moral values.

Many evolutionistic humanists regard the universe as a self-existing noncreated entity.[12] Carl Sagan even went so far as to state that "[t]he cosmos is all that there is or ever was or ever will be."[13] The *Humanist Manifestos* go on to tell us that "faith in [a] prayer hearing God… [who is] able to do something about them [prayers] is …outmoded." Not only that, but these documents maintain the position that the entire concept of salvation is "harmful [because it offers people]…false hopes of heaven."[14] This view of life causes these same evolutionists to now confidently state that "God has no role in the physical world…there is no organizing principle in the world and no purpose. Thus, *there are no moral or ethical laws that belong to the nature of things, no absolute guiding principles for human society*."[15]

Needless to say, evolutionistic humanism has not only removed God from the realm of creation, but it has removed Him from all human endeavors. Here then is the crux of their self-imposed problem. Noted humanist historians Will and Ariel Durant, the 1976 recipients of *The Humanist* magazine's Humanist Pioneer Award, have acknowledged that as humanists they "shall find it no easy task to mold a natural ethic strong enough to maintain moral restraint and social order without the support of supernatural consolations, hopes, and fears."[16] Their task however is not only difficult, I dare say it is impossible.

As historians, all they need to do is examine the aftermath of the French Revolution to see the total breakdown which occurs in a society when it attempts to live by the type of humanistic rationale expounded by today's evolutionists. For that matter, all they need do is to contemplate their own findings: "There is no significant example in history...of a society successfully maintaining moral life without the aid of religion."[17] If we can find a lesson at all in what history tells us, it is this: Every society which is based upon the philosophy of evolutionistic humanism is bound to ultimately fail because of this philosophy's internal cancer. That cancer is an absence of viable moral values and ethical standards. Such a cancer eats away at the very foundations upon which society must be based if it is going to survive.

Our forefathers had no difficulty realizing that atheistic numanism could never serve as the foundation for a system of moral values, which requires absolutes. Daniel Webster noted that

> ...our ancestors established their system of government on morality and religious sentiment. Moral

habits they believed, cannot safely be trusted on any foundation other than religious principle, nor any government be secure which is not supported by moral habits.... . Let the religious element in man's nature be neglected, let him be influenced by no higher motives than low self-interest, and subjected to no stronger restraint that the limits of civil authority and he becomes the creature of selfish passion and blind fanaticism.... . On the other hand, the cultivation of the religious sentiment represses licentiousness...inspires respect for law and order, and gives strength to the whole social fabric at the same time that it conducts the human soul upward to the Author of its being.[8]

Not only is humanistic philosophy incapable of supporting a system of absolute moral values, but it was because of this very inability that humanistic evolution caught on so quickly. When asked to give his opinion as to why it was that the notion of evolution was so readily accepted by certain segments of society, Sir Julian Huxley noted, "...the idea of God interfered with our sexual mores."[19]

It would appear that just about everyone from our founding fathers to modern-day humanistic historians have observed the chilling effect which evolutionistic humanism has upon morals and ethics. However, many evolutionists give no credence to this. Niles Eldredge does not appear to comprehend how Mrs. Niles Segraves can maintain that there is a relationship between drug abuse, prostitution, and other criminal activity and the teaching of evolution.

Mrs. Segraves is the mother of the plaintiff in what became known as the Scopes II trial. Obviously, she had taken the time to think about the logical consequences which follow from the evolutionists' line of reasoning, even if some evolutionists have not. Of what value are the virtues we know as love, charity, friendship, self-sacrifice, and loyalty? Such sentiments are nothing more than a cruel joke in a system wherein the only true reality is the survival of the fittest. If man is in fact the product of mere chance, having evolved along with the apes, the fish, the birds, and the reptiles, then his claim to life is no more secure than theirs. After all, doesn't a cattlebreeder cull his herd to eliminate unwanted strains? Thus, abortion is completely justified under this system because all that is being eliminated is "a blob of tissue" or an "unwanted animal" that possesses nothing more than the *potential* to be human. But then this system of thought does not discriminate, for it also allows for the killing off of the elderly and the mentally ill. In fact, it provided all the justification needed to kill off an entire race of people.

Hitler was an evolutionist, and he used this exact line of reasoning to eliminate 6 million human beings whom he considered genetically inferior to his master race.[20] Noted British commentator Benjamin Kidd stated that in Germany prior to World War II "Darwin's theories came to be openly set out in political and military textbooks as the full justification for war and highly organized schemes of national policy in which the doctrine of force became the doctrine of right."[21] Without a doubt, Hitler had no difficulty recognizing the point that the "ethical principle inherent in evolution is that only the best has a right to survive."[22] But then Hitler was not the only one to hold to such a perverted view of humanity.

As a boy, Joseph Stalin shared a book he had recently discovered with a young friend of his. He assured his friend that this book would show him that "all this talk about God is sheer nonsense."[23] That book was Darwin's *Origin of the Species*. It was the philosophy of evolution which Stalin used to justify the brutal imprisonment and murder of more than 4 million Russians. Stalin's actions though were merely the culmination of Lenin's beliefs, which he expressed thusly, "Darwin put an end to the belief that animal and vegetable species bear no relation to one another."[24] Just as you would discard an imperfect tomato from your garden, so also have the communists "discarded" untold millions of their own people who did not meet their standards of perfection.

Needless to say, in order for communist political systems to not only sanction these types of internal extermination programs, but actually plan them and then carry them out, their philosophical viewpoint must be devoid of any moral standards. They found justification for their position in the writings of Charles Darwin. While you may think that I am stretching things just a bit, I can assure you that I am not. All you need do is examine the facts. On December 12, 1859, Friedrich Engels wrote to Karl Marx advising him that "Darwin, whom I am just now reading, is splendid." Marx must have wholeheartedly agreed, for on December 16, 1860, he advised Engels, "...I have read all sorts of things. Among others, *Darwin's book of Natural Selection...this is the book which contains the basis in natural history for our view.*[25]

While some evolutionists would have you believe that the "social Darwinism" of Hitler, Stalin, Marx, and Engels was an outdated perversion of true evolutionistic thinking, I urge you to consider that its underlying thought process is alive and well today. Edward O. Wilson's book *Sociobiology* is filled with it. As reported in the March 13, 1989, issue of *Newsweek*, Wilson's basic premise is that man's "social behavior is shaped by the Darwinian struggle to survive and reproduce."[26] While some evolutionists are upset that such ideas are again being openly discussed, their protests have had no effect. The rationale behind the social Darwinism of the 1930's and 1940's hasn't changed at all. The only difference between then and now is that different words are being used to express the very same thoughts expressed by Hitler and Stalin.

Today Darwin's theory marches on, and as a consequence of that total lack of value it places upon human life, more than 2 million Cambodians were murdered under the regime of Pol Pot. Just as horribly though, more than 20 million American babies have been murdered in abortion mills because too many Americans have come to believe that we are mere animals as opposed to beings created in the image of Almighty God.

In addition to the relationship between the theory of evolution and genocide, Mrs. Segrave also clearly understood the relationship between evolutionary thinking and racism. Even Niles Eldredge's colleague Stephen Jay Gould, has acknowledged that "[b]iological arguments for racism may have been common before 1859, *but they increased by orders of magnitude following the acceptance of evolutionary theory*."[27] Just how blatant this racism may have become is found in a quote from the late Henry Fairfield Osborn, the evolutionistic professor of biology at Columbia University and past president of the American Museum of Natural History's board of trustees, whom we mentioned earlier in regard to our discussion of the Nebraska Man. He stated that

> The Negroid stock is even more ancient than the Caucasian...as may be proved by an examination not only of the brain, of the hair, of the bodily characteristics...but of the instincts, [and] the intelligence. The standard of intelligence of the average adult Negro is similar to that of the eleven year old youth of the species Homo Sapiens.[28]

Rather than acknowledge that there is a definite link between the evils we have just discussed and the evolutionary thought process (which by definition excludes God), the best that Eldredge could do is raise another red herring. He states that

> ...it is surely an irony that the Old Testament amply documents the presence of many of the same social ills (and plenty more) plaguing Jewish society thousands of years ago, yet nothing is said about their teaching evolution to their children.[29]

Unfortunately for him though this illustration serves only to prove my point. You see, if Mr. Eldredge had examined the Old Testament a little more closely, he would have discovered that the kingdom of Israel (both its northern and southern portions) suffered from these evils *when and only when* it abandoned the truth of God's Word and followed the false gods of its neighbors.

The problem of course is not evolution per se. Evolution is merely a symptom of the sickness, not the disease itself.

Quite simply put, where God is absent, evil rushes in to fill the vacuum. Since evolution is the foundational teaching upon which humanism must rest and humanism absolutely and unquestionably denies God, then it follows logically that where evolution and humanism are believed crime, genocide, abortion, and other evils reign supreme. And that is exactly the point Mrs. Segrave was making.

Obviously she clearly understood the relationship between the amoral teachings and situational ethics of humanism and the theory of evolution. For this she is held in disdain by a man who says that he cannot understand how ethics and evolution are related, yet himself says, "Creationism seems to me to threaten the integrity of our children's education, and this threatens the long term well being of our country."[30] As he had previously defined creationism in his book *Monkey Business* as "the belief that the cosmos, the earth, and all life are separate acts of a supernatural creator," I can only assume that he feels that by teaching our children that God's Word as recorded in the entire Bible is true, we are threatening the future of the United States of America.

Yet, look at what the evolutionists have to offer us instead: "scientists…[who] are in no position to 'prove anything' " and a system which by their own admission "can never claim to know the ultimate truth."[31] Evolutionists claim on one hand to be truth-seeking scientists and on the other that "no one has yet invented a way of determining what the truth is when we have it."[32] Perhaps it is because of statements such as these that Dr. Colin Patterson of the British Museum, who is reexamining his own position on evolution, has come to the conclusion that "evolution not only conveys no knowledge, but it seems somehow to convey anti-knowledge."[33]

To me it is interesting how evolutionists can ignore or simply forget past statements made by their heros when those comments point out their own intellectual shortcomings. For example, in all his discussion about the teaching of creationism Eldredge never once mentions the fact that Clarence Darrow, the ACLU attorney who represented the *evolutionists'* position in the original Scopes trial, stated that it is the height of "bigotry for public schools to teach only one theory of origins."[34] Even Darwin acknowledged that "[a] fair result can be obtained only by stating and balancing the facts and arguments on both sides of each question... ."[35] Since most evolutionists clearly insist that *only* evolution be taught to today's students, they have by their own words placed themselves in a position which Darrow classified as bigoted and Darwin contended was unfair.

The evolutionists' own statements regarding what science is point out yet another area which contradicts the "simple to complex" premise of evolution. This area deals with the development of language. Evolution would tell us that man could barely speak when he first appeared. He then slowly evolved into the supposedly highly articulate, intellectually superior evolutionists which we see today. Yet, linguistic research has shown that there is "no tribe or people anywhere in the world which does not have thousands of words in its vocabulary and an intricate systematic way of putting words together into phrases and sentences."[36]

What we find when we examine even supposedly primitive tribes is that their language, which appears rather simple at first, is more often than not the remains of a more intricate, complex pattern of speech which that tribe's ancestors had used. As the functions of that particular culture disappeared, the words and phrases of the past civilization which had described these functions were dropped.[37] Again, we see the breakdown of something, not its evolution. The evidence simply does not establish a general pattern of simple to complex. While it is true that new words may be coined to define new ideas or inventions, it is also true that taken as a whole the language in which this occurs actually becomes less complex at the same time. English is a perfect example of this phenomenon.

In addition, linguists have also discovered that there is no evidence of any common source or historical connection between any of the 50 distinct families of languages which exist in the world today. Remember, this is in spite of the fact that it has been demonstrated that man had a single place of origin. The fact that no common link exists between these families of languages tends to support not the theory of evolution, but the biblical account of Genesis chapter 11, wherein we are shown that God totally confused the languages of the world at the Tower of Babel.

The process of language deterioration continues on to this day. We need look no further than the "science" of evolution to establish this principle. When I was in school I was taught that science was the study of natural phenomena. *Possible* explanations for the occurrence of these phenomena were proposed as *hypotheses*. After initial testing appeared to verify a hypothesis, it was upgraded to the status of *theory*.

After years of testing by men of science throughout the world who used universally accepted procedures and found no exceptions to the theory, it was called a *fact*. My *American College Dictionary* still carries these different definitions. Eldredge however states that "philosophers of science have argued long and hard over the difference between facts, hypotheses, and theories. But the real point is this: *they are all essentially the same, all of them are ideas... ."*[38]

As we have so graphically seen, the evolutionists have completely altered the idea of what the truth is, something every humanist must do in order to justify the situational ethics he expounds. Now they are diluting the very language which serves as the basis for modern science. Having diluted the language of science to nothing more than a series of meaningless interchangeable words (which after all is exactly what the deterioration of language does), evolutionists now feel secure in making the following statement: "...[T]he earth simply cannot be a mere ten thousand years old. This is no story concocted by a Creator as part of his creation process. The earth really is incredibly old. And of course the universe is even older—15 billion years or so."[39] They can also readily assert that "precious few ideas put forth to date in science have entirely withstood the test of time. Evolution is one, so is the idea that the earth is round... . Evolution is a fact as much as the idea that the earth is shaped like a ball."[40]

When language begins to deteriorate, as the evidence shows that it has, it is a mixed blessing. In this case it serves as additional proof that Darwinian evolution did not occur. However, by using their watered-down definition for the word *fact*, the evolutionist feels perfectly free in calling evolution a fact. In reality, Darwinian evolution is nothing more than a hypothesis, and a philosophical one at that.

The evolutionists' attack on the English language goes even further. After making such a preposterous statement as "evolution is a fact as much as the idea that the earth is shaped like a ball," Eldredge attempts to give the impression of impartiality. He does so by asserting that "the *notion* of evolution is falsifiable—we can theoretically throw it out should evidence one day point that way."[41] This statement is misleading because it conceals the fact that as far as he is concerned there is no way evolution could be proven false. By equating the roundness of the earth with the theory of evolution he has pointed out the total inflexibility of his mind set. (Remember, it was this same type of inflexibility which led his predecessors to make false statements concerning the lack of transitional evidence in the fossil record.)

Eldredge's statements however serve as further evidence of the watering down of scientific terms. As we saw previously, he felt no hesitancy about interchanging the words *hypothesis* and *theory* with the word *fact*, but now he does the same thing with the word *notion* and *fact*. First we are told that evolution is a *fact*, and then we are told that it is a *notion*. Returning to my dictionary for a moment, I discover that a *notion* is a "more or less general, vague, imperfect conception or idea of something...an opinion, view, or belief." If Mr. Eldredge would accept the dictionary definition of the word *notion*, then I would acknowledge evolution as a notion, for it most certainly is an imperfect conception of the origins of the species, which requires a great deal of belief.

Chapter 7

Higher Education

The United States may well be in jeopardy of destruction from within. However, that situation has arisen not from teaching the truths of God's Word, but from our failure to insist that our education system *continue* to do that which it had done from its very inception.

> The moral principles and precepts contained in the Scripture ought to form the basis of all our civil constitutions and laws. All the miseries and evils which men suffer from—vice, crime, ambition, injustice, oppression, slavery, and war—proceed from their despising or neglecting the precepts contained in the Bible.[1]

That quote came not from Mrs. Segrave, but from Noah Webster in 1828.

While evolutionists will tell you that they accept the biblical precepts of moral goodness, I remind you that nowhere in the Bible does it tell us to believe only that part of it which we want—and to reject the rest. Among the precepts contained in the Bible is the unquestionable integrity of God's Word. Perhaps I should not use the word *unquestionable*, for there can be no doubt that evolution in particular and secular humanism in general has questioned God's integrity. In addition to calling the Genesis account of creation a "concoction," at least one prominent evolutionist has referred to this integrity as nothing more than "the wisdom and world view of a near eastern culture thousands of years old."[2]

While evolutionists are indeed entitled to their own opinions of the Bible, I wonder if they are aware of the fact that their opinions run contrary to those held by the very men who have shaped this country. John Quincy Adams said, "The first and almost the only book deserving of universal attention is the Bible." Andrew Jackson was of the opinion that "[T]he Scriptures [form]...the rock on which our Republic rests." U.S. Grant observed that "The Bible is the sheetanchor of our liberties." Horace Greeley even went so far as to publicly state, "It is impossible to enslave mentally or socially, a Bible reading people. The principles of the Bible are the groundwork of human freedom." Woodrow Wilson viewed the Bible as "the one supreme source of revelation of the meaning of life, the nature of God and spiritual nature, and the needs of men." Concerning the future stability of this country and that stability's relationship to the Bible, Calvin Coolidge spoke in words which even an evolutionist could not misconstrue: "The foundations of our society and our government rest so much on the teachings of the Bible that it would be difficult to support them if faith in these teachings would cease to be practically universal in our country."[3]

We are told in Second Chronicles 7:14, "...if **My** people...will humble themselves and pray and seek **My face** and turn from their wicked ways, then I will hear from heaven and will forgive their sin and will heal their land." God's promise to heal the land is conditional in nature. Before the healing process can begin we must humble ourselves, pray, and seek God's face. Even though evolutionists refuse to recognize this fact, it was common knowledge among our nation's greatest leaders.

While I wish I could claim to be the author of the following words, all I can do is repeat them for you and allow you to ponder them in your heart:

> We have grown in numbers, wealth, and power as no other nation has ever grown. But we have forgotten God. We have forgotten the gracious hand which preserves us in peace, and multiplied and enriched and strengthened us; as we have vainly imagined, in the deceitfulness of our hearts, that all these blessings were produced by some superior wisdom and virtue of our own. Intoxicated with unbroken success we have become too self-sufficient to feel the necessity of redeeming and preserving grace; too proud to *pray to the God that made us.* It behooves us then to humble ourselves before the offended power to confess our national sins and to pray for clemency and forgiveness.

Those words are taken from the Presidential Proclamation Appointing a National Fast Day. The president who made this proclamation on March 30, 1963, was Abraham Lincoln.[4] After the Civil War Robert E. Lee echoed the thoughts of his former adversary with these words: "...knowing that intercessory prayer is our mightiest weapon and the supreme call for all Christians today...[l]et us pray for our nation...for those who have never known Jesus Christ...for our nation's leaders..... Let prayer be our passion. Let prayer be our practice."[5]

Again, the very premise of the evolutionist is false. Our national tragedy is not the fact that more and more Americans are insisting that God's Word be taught as true, but that we ever allowed something (evolution) which calls itself science (when in reality it is merely another religion) to ever take the place of God's Word in the first place. Allow me to point out the observation of Mr. Charles Malik, a former president of the United Nations General Assembly, which came from a conversation he had with then U.S. Secretary of State Cyrus Vance. In response to a question as to what was wrong with the United States, Mr. Malik stated, "You have taken Jesus Christ out of your universities."[6]

It is not the fact that many people are desirous of having their children taught the truths of God's Word which has seriously eroded the moral fabric of this country; it is the fact that the educational system of this country has forgotten the admonition of the very founders of such great universities as Harvard which directed its students to "know God and Jesus Christ...as the only foundation for all sound knowledge and learning."[7] Our system of education has failed to live up to the purpose for which institutions of higher education such as Columbia University were created, that is, "To teach and encourage students to know God in Jesus Christ and to love and serve Him...with a perfect and willing mind."[8] We have lost track of the fact that major universities such as Yale were once described as, "...a little temple [where] prayer and praise seem to be the delight of the greater part of the students."[9]

As a nation we have forgotten the fact that of the first 119 colleges and universities founded in the United States, 104 of them were created for the purpose of teaching their students about the Creator and His creations.[10] In fact, the Bible was considered such an integral part of our educational heritage that Noah Webster was merely expressing a commonly accepted fact when he said, "...education is useless without the Bible."[11]

We must never forget that Fisher Ames, the *founding father who actually wrote the First Amendment*, expressed his belief that the Bible was to play a prominent role in *public education* when he said,

> It has been the custom of late years, to put a number of little books into the hands of children, containing fables and moral lessons. Why then, if these books for children must be retained,...should not the Bible regain the place it once held as a school book? Its morals are pure, its examples captivating and noble. The reverence for the sacred book that is thus impressed lasts long...[T]he Bible will justly remain the standard of language as well as of faith.[12]

We must never forget that when he was president, Thomas Jefferson also served as superintendent of schools for Washington,

D.C., and that as superintendent he declared that the Bible was to be the primary reading text for its students.[13]

We must never forget that Congress also recognized the importance of religion in American education life when in 1787 and again in 1789, under the terms of the Northwest Ordinance, it set aside *federal* land for schools using the following rationale:

> *Religion*, morality, and knowledge being necessary to good government and the happiness of mankind, schools and the means of learning shall forever be encouraged.

Note also that this was at a time when the vast majority of all schools in the United States were run by the Church. Furthermore, no portion of the Northwest Territory could apply for statehood if its proposed constitution prohibited the teaching of religion and morality in its public schools. Remember also that the Congress which passed the Northwest Ordinance was the very Congress which passed the First Amendment.

We must not forget that the preamble to one of the earliest *public* education laws in the colonies stated in 1647 that the purpose of education was primarily spiritual when it acknowledged that

> …it being one chief project of…Satan, to keep men from the knowledge of ye Scriptures…[people must be certain] that learning may not be buried in ye grave.[14]

We must not forget that some of our colonial ancestors' concepts concerning education were formed by reading the works of such men as John Locke, who made the following statement:

> There ought very early to be imprinted on his [a child's] mind a true notion of God, as the independent Supreme Being, Author and Maker of all things, from whom we receive all our good, and who loves and gives us all things.... . [T]he Lord's prayer, the creeds, and Ten Commandments, tis necessary he should learn perfectly by heart.[15]

We must not forget that the philosophy of education shared by our founding fathers was best summed up by Samuel Adams on October 4, 1790, when he said,

> Let divines and philosophers, statesmen, and patriots unite their endeavors to renovate the age, by impressing the minds of men with the importance of educating their little boys and girls, of inculcating in the minds of youth the fear and love of the Deity and universal philanthropy.... . In short, of leading them in the study and practice of the exalted virtues of the Christian system.[16]

We must not forget that this educational system (mostly Church-sponsored) was apparently quite successful, for John Adams noted in 1765 that "[A] native of America who cannot read or write is as rare as a comet or an earthquake."[17]

We must not forget that this remained the case well into the 19th century, when it was noted by the French historian Alexis de Tocqueville in 1848 that

> America is still the place where the Christian religion has kept the greatest real power over men's souls.

Nothing better demonstrates how useful and natural it is to men, since the country where it now has the widest sway is both the *most enlightened* and the freest.[18]

We must not forget that the *New England Primer*, America's first textbook, taught the ABC's to our children using these examples:

A. In *Adam's* fall we sinned all.
B. Heaven to find, the *Bible* mind.
C. *Christ* crucify'd for sinners dy'd.[19]

We must not forget that McGuffey's readers, which were used to teach 120 million Americans to read, contained this statement: "The Ten Commandments and the teachings of Jesus Christ are not only basic, but plenary... ."[20]

All this clearly serves to show us that it is not the fact that religion *is* being taught in our public schools that has brought us to the state we are in, it is the fact that we have exchanged the God of our forefathers for the religion of secular humanism and its cornerstone teaching of Darwinian evolution.

At this point there should be no doubt in the reader's mind that the foundations of this country's educational system were Christian. Nor should there be any doubt that this system performed admirably. It is regrettable that we are no longer teaching our children under this system. In fact, as of November 17, 1980, it is supposedly unconstitutional for the same Ten Commandments which McGuffey's reader said were plenary to a child's education even to be posted on the schoolhouse wall.[21] Since the mid 1940's we have slowly but surely been replacing this God-centered educational system with an amoral humanistic one. What have been the results of this switch? Following are merely two of them: The crime rate in the Los Angeles public school system became so bad that then attorney general for California, George Deukmejian, filed suit against the local school board. In so doing he maintained that to force students to attend those schools was tantamount to inflicting cruel and unusual punishment upon them.[22]

Not only are many public schools unsafe, but most have not been able to fulfill what has historically been considered their primary responsibility, that of teaching Dick and Jane to read. This failure has been so complete that as of 1975 the U.S. Department of Health, Education, and Welfare estimated that 20 percent of our adult population lacked the basic skills necessary to even function in everyday life. Today there are over 23 million adults in this country who are functionally illiterate. However, things aren't faring much better for school children either. Forty percent of our grade school graduates are unable to read material of an appropriate grade level. Eighty percent of these same children cannot even write a simple descriptive paragraph.[23] Our current public school system is in such a shambles that one national educator was quoted as saying that if an enemy had done to our schools what we have done to our schools, it would have been considered an act of war. Yet this is the same system which the evolutionists want to not only maintain, but pump even more money into.

While this state of affairs is indeed deplorable, it should come as no surprise. This is especially so when we consider the source of the educational philosophy which has governed our public school system during the last half of this century. John Dewey (1859–1952) is considered to be the father of what has unfortunately been called our modern system of "progressive" education. According to Will Durant, *"The starting point of his [Dewey's] system of thought is biological: he sees man as an organism in an environment...[Dewey believed that] things are to be understood through their origins...without the intrusions of supernatural considerations.* "[24] However, few of us realize that Dewey was also one of the authors and signers of the "Humanist Manifesto."

What these two facts reveal is that the humanistic/ evolutionistic viewpoint which has permeated our public schools is the very same anti-Christian philosophy which, as we saw earlier in this study, is totally incapable of supporting the morals and ethics which are essential if a society is to remain healthy and vibrant. Not only that, but through a process known as "values clarification" the public schools have actively sought to undermine what remains of the Judeo/Christian ethic which has served this country so well since its very inception.

Just in case you may be under the impression that values clarification is nothing more than a harmless philosophical exercise, I wish to remind you that according to humanists, "...moral values derive their source from human experience. Ethics...[are] situational, needing no theological or ideological sanction.[25] You see, humanists do not want the absolute Christian values which served as the foundation upon which this country was built "clarified," i.e., made perfectly clear in the student's mind. They want these ethics expunged and replaced with their own. Again, just in case you feel that I may be stretching the point a bit, I suggest that you ponder carefully the implications of this statement by Harvard professor emeritus Joseph Fletcher, author of the book *Situation Ethics*:

> Whether we ought to follow a moral principle or not would, I contend, *always depend upon the situation...* If we are, as I would want to reason, obliged in conscience sometimes to engage in white lies, as we often call them, then in conscience we might be obliged sometimes to engage in white thefts, and white fornications, and white killings, and white breaking of promises, and the like.[26]

In this report entitled "Schooling for the Future," Dr. John Goodlad of the National Educational Association boldly stated, "Our goal is behavioral change. The majority of our youth still hold to the values of their parents, if we do not resocialize them to accept change, our society will decay."[27]

The foregoing is not meant to serve as an indictment of those open-minded, truth-seeking public school teachers who are sincerely attempting to present all sides of the origins issue. It is however intended to point out in no uncertain terms that the evolutionistic/humanistic philosophy which controls our schools is anything but neutral when it comes to religion. Humanism's strong anti-Christian position is clearly spelled out in the following quote from an article entitled "A Religion for a New Age," which appeared in the January/February 1983 issue of *The Humanist* magazine:

> [T]he battle for humankind's future must be waged and won in the public school classroom by teachers

who correctly perceive their role as proselytizers of a new faith: a religion of humanity... . These teachers must embody the same selfless dedication as the most rabid fundamentalist preachers, for they will be ministers of another sort, utilizing a classroom instead of a pulpit to convey humanist values in whatever subject they teach, regardless of the educational level—preschool day care or large university. The classroom must and will become an arena of conflict between...the rotting corpse of Christianity, together with all its adjacent evils and misery, and the new faith of humanism... .[28]

In spite of all this, evolutionists insist that if the creationists are successful in turning our schools around they will be establishing "the groundwork for legally enforced ignorance and totalitarian thought control."[29] On one hand, the facts clearly show that our God-centered educational system produced the most enlightened and freest populace which the world had ever seen. On the other hand, they reveal that the atheistic/evolutionistic thought process which currently controls public education in this country has produced the highest level of illiteracy and ignorance in our history. Yet, humanists do not want us to return to our Christian educational roots because, if we do, they think we will end up with the same tragic results which our current atheistic system has already achieved!

Such thinking may make sense in Alice's wonderland or Orwell's animal farm; however, I do not find it particularly compelling. But then I am honestly concerned about the sad state of public education in this country, whereas many evolutionistic humanists leave the clear impression that for them the most important aspect of public education has nothing to do with "teaching" our children, as that concept has been traditionally understood. As a case in point, note the thoughts of humanist scholar Paul Blanshard:

> I think the most important factor moving us toward a secular society has been the educational factor. Our schools may not teach Johnny to read properly, but the fact that Johnny is in school until he is sixteen tends to lead toward the elimination of religious superstition.... This mitigates against Adam and Eve and all other myths of alleged history.... Humanism as a scholarly substitute for religious mythology is quietly gaining ground.[30]

Unfortunately for today's students though, the inroads made by this philosophy of humanism have come about at the expense of academic integrity. Not only do these evolutionistic humanists purposefully ignore the scientific facts which disprove their theory, but they are rewriting our very history by eliminating virtually all references to Christianity from many textbooks. If you are under the impression that this simply is not so, then consider the words of one professor of education at Harvard University:

> Every child in America entering school at the age of five is mentally ill because he comes to school with certain allegiances toward our founding fathers, toward our elected officials, toward his parents, toward a belief in a supernatural Being, toward the sovereignty of this nation as a separate entity. It is up to you

teachers to make all these sick children well by creating the international child of the future.[31]

Eldredge closed his discussion on the plight of the American education system with this warning,"…scientific illiteracy will send the United States on a surer and straighter path to hell than ever will the idea called evolution."[32] As we saw earlier, he equated the potential downfall of the United States with creationism, but now he equates its salvation with his brand of science.

There can be no doubt that in a technological society such as ours science (true science, that is) is important. But there is a vast difference between the scientific world of experimentation and the evolutionary world of conjecture. Dr. Randall Susman, an evolutionistic anthropologist with the University of New York at Stony Brook, acknowledged that "We go about things indirectly, and as a result its *open to a lot more error* than sciences where you have experimentation."[33] What's more is that David Philbeam, Harvard University's top evolutionary anthropologist, recently conceded that this conjecture has played a major role in his field of study: "I know that at least in paleontology…theory heavily influences interpretations. *Theories* have in the past, *clearly reflected our current ideologies, instead of actual data.*"[34] While he is himself a dedicated evolutionist, Dr. Robert Bakker of the University of Colorado also recently acknowledged that even today many of his colleagues still allow their preconceived notions to influence their actions and statements. Apparently he recognizes the fact that in reality such thinking represents the very antithesis of true science. He even went so far as to refer to such thinking as "pretzel logic."[35]

Needless to say, there is a vast difference between true science and evolution. There is also a vast difference between the discoveries cautiously announced by the scientific world of experimentation and the Olympian pronouncements made by many in the evolutionary community. It was not until after three years of careful research and testing that Louis Pasteur was willing to make public his discovery of a possible treatment for rabies. Even then it was only after he was faced with a life or death situation for a young boy.[36] On the other hand, we have Richard Leakey, who on *Friday*, August 27, 1982, found a jawbone in the hills of western Kenya and on *Tuesday*, August 31, *only four days later*, held a news conference and announced, "We consider it a critical specimen...we expect to find it about 8 million years old. It fills that fossil gap."[37]

However, we should not be surprised by such declarations. Leakey shares a common preconceived notion with most evolutionists. He openly admits "I find it very strange that today many people still think of evolution as just a theory...there is sufficient evidence to demonstrate evolution as a fact... . We're here as a result of a series of accidents. There is nothing pre-planned about humanity."[38] Remember now, this statement is made in spite of the fact that, as we have so clearly seen, the evidence in question does not support the theory of evolution. What this evidence does support though is the proposition that the evolutionists' preconceived notion that evolution is a fact has caused them to ignore, misrepresent, or misinterpret virtually every anthropological, archaeological, or biological discovery since Darwin first proposed his hypothesis.

In spite of the fact that some evolutionists will now admit that they rely more on hindsight than they do on equations,[39] evolutionists are determined in their efforts to equate the theory of evolution (in all its variant forms) with true science. At the same time they label the creationists' viewpoint as religious.[40] By doing this, they hope to keep any talk of creationism from entering into the science classroom. They seek to protect their brand of science from the damaging influences which they think the creationist's thought process might inflict. They do this even if, as Dr. Robert Jastrow pointed out, they must ignore the very evidence for creation which they themselves have uncovered.

Just what do you suppose would happen to today's public school science classroom if members of the evolutionary community honestly evaluated their position? The answer to that question was given by Dr. Colin Patterson during his keynote address at Eldredge's own American Museum of Natural History on November 5, 1981. As you read this astounding quote keep in mind the fact that these are not the words of a creationist, but those of a man who has defended the evolutionists' position for more than 20 years.

One of the reasons I started taking this antievolutionary view, or let's call it a nonevolutionary view, was last year I had a sudden realization for over 20 years I thought I had been working on evolution in some way. One morning I woke up and something had happened in the night, and it struck me that *I had been working on this stuff for 20 years and there was not one thing I knew about it.* That's quite a shock to learn that one can be so misled so long. Either there was something wrong with me or there was something wrong with evolutionary theory. Naturally, I know there is nothing wrong with me, so for the last few weeks I've tried putting a simple question to various people and groups of people.

Question is, can you tell me anything you know about evolution, any one thing, anything that is true? I tried that question on the geology staff at the Field Museum of Natural History and the only answer I got was silence. I tried it on members of the Evolutionary Morphology Seminar in the University of Chicago, a very prestigious body of evolutionists, and all I got there was silence for a long time, and eventually one person said, *"I do know one thing—it ought not to be taught in high school."*[41]

As I said at the outset of this study, I am not against science. Nor am I against any evolutionist believing what he wants to believe or even expounding upon it in some course on comparative religions or philosophy. At least in 306 B.C., Epicurus was honest enough to call his theory of the chance creation of life a "philosophy." Christianity has been confronted with the task of refuting those who believe in the chance creation of the world ever since the apostle Paul first met epicurean philosophers (see Acts 17:18-24).

Some of those highly educated men belittled Paul by asking, "What is this babbler trying to say?" Today's epicurean philosophers, otherwise known as "evolutionistic scientists," also taunt Christians. All to often they prefer character assassination to an honest discussion of the issues. To quote Stephen Jay Gould, "Creationist bashing is a noble and necessary pursuit these days."[42] Rather than address the facts, they accuse us of having committed intellectual suicide when we accept the Genesis account of creation. However, I ask you to consider the possibility that it is not the Christian who is guilty of this self-inflicted crime. The Bible after all has not been proven wrong by true science. Numerous times archaeologists and historians thought that the Bible was wrong, but each time further investigation and subsequent discoveries have proven the biblical account to be accurate. However, the evolutionists have been forced to abandon all three major tenets of Darwin's theory less than a hundred years after it was proposed, namely the gradual evolution of all species, geologic uniformitarianism, and the simultaneous initial appearance of mankind at numerous locations throughout the earth. Needless to say, the facts clearly show that the biblical record of accuracy clearly exceeds that of Darwinian evolution.

Chapter 8

IQ Test

Let's engage in one final intellectual exercise. For various reasons Christians who accept the biblical account of the great flood are considered naive. Let's take a look at just a few of those reasons and see what the facts really reveal. Some people say that Noah's ark was too small to hold all those animals. However, using even the smallest estimate of what a cubit was, we find the ark contained approximately 1 million 396 thousand cubic feet of space; it was divided into three decks and displaced about 20 thousand tons of water (see Gen. 6:14-16). All told, it is estimated that Noah would have had to accommodate about 17 thousand pairs of animals, birds, reptiles, and amphibians on board the ark. Keep in mind that there was no requirement that the elephants, giraffes, hippopotami, and yes, probably even the dinosaurs, had to be adult in size, only that they had to be male and female. Even if they were all adults, the average size of the combined population would be approximately that of a sheep. In that case they would all fit into the space of 146 two-tiered stock transport cars. Since the ark was large enough to hold 522 such stockcars, the amount of supplies for which they had room would be equal to that which could be carried in 376 such cars. So much for the inadequate space argument.[1]

Others have argued that the flood was only a local inundation. However, such an assertion does not fit with the biblical account, which specifically says that the waters *covered* the tops of the mountains to a depth of more than 20 feet. That statement alone makes it worldwide in scope, but then so do the statements found in Second Peter 3:6, Hebrews 11:7, First Peter 3:20, and Jesus' own words in Luke 17:27. Those who believe in only a local deluge also ignore the fact that, while details may be different, the history of every culture which can be traced back to the approximate time of the flood mentions a worldwide flood. These cultures were originated by the descendants of Noah and were scattered throughout the earth after their language was confused at the Tower of Babel. As each culture drifted further and further away from worshiping the one true God who created us all, their versions of the flood likewise drifted further and further from the true account as contained in Genesis.

Still, other people have said that not enough water would have been available to cover the whole earth. However, since 71 percent of the earth's surface is currently covered with water to an average depth of 12,500 feet, and there is a great deal of water stored in the polar ice caps (which weren't always frozen), and the waters of the flood came up from the deep and down from the atmosphere, there would have been more than enough water to cover the world.

Two things need to be noted in this regard. First, the atmosphere may well have contained much more water than it does now in the form of a vapor canopy. Second, the mountain ranges may well have been lower prior to the flood than they are now; therefore, less water would have been needed to cover the tops of the mountains in the prediluvian age. (See the Scripture references following point 5 below.)

Finally, many people have wondered how the animals would have overcome their natural fear of man and voluntarily come to Noah. The answer is found in Genesis 9:2, which tells us that animals did not have a "natural" fear of man until after the flood. We also need to bear in mind that the rest of Genesis tells us that God led the animals to Noah.

So much for some of the more prominent objections which are raised by skeptics. Now, let's take a quick look at merely a few of the geological and paleontological problems which the evolutionists cannot answer, but which are answered by the Genesis account of the flood.

1. The flood would explain the sudden disappearance of hundreds of species which failed to adapt to the great climatic changes which occurred after the flood. (The dinosaurs would of course be a prime example of this.)

2. The disappearance of the vapor canopy, which previously had provided a natural greenhouse effect on the Earth, would explain the geological evidence of a tropical climate which was universal until after the flood.

3. The flood would explain the size of the otherwise inexplicably huge fossil beds found in Africa, Sicily, and numerous other locations.

4. The weight of all that extra water on the earth's surface could easily account for the vertical drops measured in miles, as previously mentioned by Dr. Landes.

5. The geologic upheaval which took place during the flood and shortly thereafter as the world settled down would serve as a logical explanation for the location of marine fossils on mountain tops, the apparently young age of many mountain ranges, and the unbroken wave pattern which appears in many rock layers. This pattern could not have been formed in "solid" rock unless the rock layers in which these patterns appear had been in a liquid, gel-like or pliable condition when the layers moved, which is the state they would have been in immediately after the flood. Remember, 75 percent of the rock found on the continents is sedimentary rock, which is rock that has been laid down by water.

Concerning the mountain-building which took place during or immediately after the flood, note Psalm 104:8 as translated in either the RSV, NAS, TLB, or ML versions. (While not directly related to the flood, please note also that the continental drift need not have taken hundreds of millions of years to accomplish, but may well have occurred either during the life of Peleg, "...because in his time the earth was divided" (Gen. 10:25), or following and as a direct result of the geologic upheaval associated with the upsurge of the fountains of the deep.)

6. The suddenness of the climatic change after the flood would explain the quick-frozen condition of the Siberian mammoths—something no ice age theory has satisfactorily accounted for.

7. The mysterious fossil finds of Leakey and others would suggest the very sudden burial of many soft-bodied creatures in a substance other than hot lava or ash, hence their remarkable state of preservation.

8. The flood would also explain the massive simultaneous burial of the billions of tons of vegetation necessary to account for the coal and the simultaneous burial of the billions of animals necessary to account for the oil which is found in the earth today. Note that it doesn't take millions of years for coal to form. It has been formed in laboratories in a few minutes.[2] Oil has been produced from organic material in fewer than six years under controlled conditions[3] and is acknowledged by modern geologists to have been formed naturally in as little as a few thousand years.[4]

9. The massive geological formations such as the Deccan Plateau of India could most reasonably be explained by the major upheaval of such a catastrophic flood.

This list goes on and on.[5] The point is the Genesis account of the flood provides us with sensible answers to questions which hadn't even been asked when the Bible was written, whereas evolutionists cannot yet provide answers to the questions they themselves have asked. All the philosophy of evolution can do is give conflicting answers to some, ignore others, and call the remainder of them mysteries. Now I ask you, which is the intellectual approach?

Intellectually speaking, the integrity, uniformity, and accuracy of the Bible is better established than for any book found in the entire collection of books known as *The Great Books of the Western World*. The Bible was written over a period of 1,500 years, with God using more than 40 writers from all walks of life. He used a king and a shepherd, a general and a fisherman, a statesman, and a servant, a tent-making rabbi and a gentile doctor, and a prophet and a tax collector. It was written in three languages on three continents during times of war and during times of peace; yet, its uniformity when dealing with the most controversial subjects ever to face mankind is unparalleled by any book, philosophy, or science ever devised by man.

Some professors who are considered intellectual readily accept the authorship, philosophical content, and in some cases the literal historical accuracy of Homer's *Iliad*, yet scoff at the integrity of the Bible. But consider this: The *Iliad* was written in 900 B.C.; the earliest known copy of it comes from 400 B.C. This means that of the more than 643 earliest copies or portions of copies of the *Iliad* which exist today, none were made earlier than five hundred years after the original was penned by Homer himself. On the other hand, the books which comprise the New Testament were written between 40 A.D. and 100 A.D.; the earliest copies or fragments of copies in existence today come from 124 A.D. That gives us a span of only 25 years from the original to the existing copies as compared to the five hundred years for the *Iliad*. Now I ask you, which one has the greatest chance of containing transcription error?

Furthermore, there are over 24 thousand ancient copies or portions of the New Testament as opposed to only 643 copies or portions of the *Iliad*. Yet the *Iliad* is considered to be the most authenticated piece of ancient literature (aside from the Bible) that ever was written. Remember Lucretius, the

Roman poet/philosopher, who was cited approvingly by the evolutionist Gavin deBeer? His writings are verifiable only from two known early manuscripts, and the earliest of these is a copy made a thousand years after he died. In spite of these facts the "intellectual evolutionists" give more credence to the works of Lucretius than they do to the Word of God.

To the truth-seeking, open-minded individual who accepts the theory of evolution I ask this favor. Before you give any more credence to those who dismiss the Bible as nothing more than the wisdom of a Near Eastern culture thousands of years removed from modern man, read a book entitled *Evidence That Demands a Verdict* by Josh McDowell. I have no association with Mr. McDowell whatsoever; however, I refer to this book because of the depth of research and easily verifiable references contained therein. Of course, I would rather have you refer directly to the Bible, but if you do not feel that you can intellectually do so until after you have verified it to a greater extent than any book ever written has been verified, read McDowell's book.

First Corinthians 2:14 tells us, "The man without the Spirit does not accept the things that come from the Spirit of God, for they are foolishness to him, and he cannot understand them... ." While the things of God are indeed foolishness to the man who denies God's existence,the wisdom of such a man is foolishness to God (see 1 Cor. 3:19). Allow me to point out one other example of the foolish statements made by evolutionists. In one breath they say they accept the moral principles found in the Bible, yet by denying the Genesis account of creation they are calling the author of those principles a liar!

To any proponent of the theory of evolution who has read this far, I would like to say that this book has not been written to attack any person, but rather an idea. The apostle Paul asked this question in Galatians 4:16, "Have I now become your enemy by telling you the truth?" It is not my desire that you and I be enemies. It is however my desire for you to know the truth. In this case, the truth is crystal clear, the idea of Darwinian evolution is diametrically opposed to God's Word, and its prime purpose is eliminating from your mind your need for a personal Savior. As we have already seen, it is doing this by deceiving you into thinking that you are getting better and better. It is telling you that you can overcome all things solely by looking deep within yourself and then drawing upon that which is in you and all mankind. However, unless that which is in you is Jesus Christ, you will eventually fail.

The theory of evolution is merely a natural outcome of the religion/philosophy of secular humanism. Philosophies themselves are the direct result of the failure of our sensory knowledge to find true reality in life. Since these philosophies deny the existence of the God of creation whom they can neither see, feel, taste, hear, nor smell, they have come up with their own explanations for life's purpose, functions, goals, and origins. Yet, they all contradict each other.

What's more regrettable for those who cling to these ideas though is the fact that they have all failed to give true, lasting meaning to life. The evolutionist/humanist philosopher is like the undertaker who covers the casket with flowers to hide that which is concealed within. Evolutionists seek to hide their failure to give purpose to life, let alone explain its origins, by using flowery language. But as is true with the undertaker, once you get past all the pretty flowers and look closely at what is really there, all you find is death. It could well be your soul that is lying there. Jesus Christ, and only Jesus Christ, is the way, the truth, and the life (see Jn. 3:18; 14:6).

I ask you to consider this. If you are right, and I am wrong in my assertion that there not only is a Creator God, but this Creator is the one true God as recorded in Genesis, then as both you and I stand together facing eternity, we will do so on an equal footing. However, if you are wrong, and I am indeed correct, we will still face eternity together, but we will no longer be on an equal footing. The very God whom you denied will say to *me*, "Well done, thou good and faithful servant"" (Mt. 25:21, KJV).But because He is the God of truth and justice, as well as the God of creation, He will say to *you* who denied Him, "Depart from Me,…into eternal fire…"(Mt. 25:41).

Please do not tell me that a really loving God would not do that. Such a statement is the result of taking only part of what the Bible tells us about God and ignoring the rest. You see, He is the God of love, but He is also just. He showed His love for all men by sending Jesus Christ to die for us. He has said that salvation is available to all who come to Him through Jesus, and since He is just and does not lie, that is the *only* way to salvation (see Jn. 14:6; 8:24; Acts 4:12; 1 John 5:12; Jn. 3:18). Are you now willing to stake the well-being of your soul upon a theory which is as changing as the shifting sand? I shall pray that you are not so inclined. I do so not from any position of self-righteousness or arrogance, but from a sincere desire that you and I will indeed face eternity together standing on the Rock of Jesus Christ. That desire comes not from within myself, but from the very God who created you and me.

If you are a deistic evolutionist who accepts the theory that there is a God who at the very outset created that initial particle of matter from which the whole universe arose, you are now faced with this question, Who is this God? In the past you may have ignored that question, but you cannot now ignore it and remain intellectual. No religion on earth allows you that option, except secular humanism, which says that man is his own god, and we both know that neither you nor I created that initial particle.

Muslims, Hindus, Jehovah's Witnesses, Mormons, and Christian Scientists, to name merely a few, all accept Jesus Christ as either a prophet, divine teacher, a god (with a lower case *g*), one of many gods, or a great man; but they each deny that He is, along with the Father and the Holy Spirit, the one true God. However, that is exactly who He said He was (see Jn. 5:18; Mt. 1:23; 28:19; Jn. 10:30,33; 17:11; Col. 2:9; Jn. 1:1; Rev. 1:17 with Is. 44:6; Rev. 2:23 with Jer. 17:10). Therefore, since the aforementioned religions deny that He is who He said He was, they are calling Him a liar. At the same time however they accept Him as either a prophet, divine teacher, god, one of many gods, or a great man. They say he is not God, although He says He is. However, they still pay Him a great deal of homage. Now, I ask you, can you accept a belief system which gives such great honor to a man who it claims is a liar? Both the intelligent answer and the biblical answer have to be no. You see, the truly intelligent answer and the biblical answer are never at odds with each other. That does not mean that the biblical answer is always the obvious answer, but then neither is the intelligent one.

You are now face to face with the issue that those other religions attempt to sidestep by relegating Jesus to a rule other than the one which is rightfully His (Col. 1:17-20 and 2:9). You must either accept Him for what He is or call Him a liar. In addition to being the Savior whom the Father sent to die for our sins, Jesus claims to be the Creator, and He claims that He created in exactly the same way that Genesis chapter 1 and 2 tell us that He did. If you deny that, then you have placed yourself in the same position as an atheistic evolutionists, namely, you have denied God by calling Him a liar.

I would therefore ask you what I earlier asked the evolutionist to consider. Are you willing to stake your soul upon the theory of evolution? For you that would be an even less intelligent choice than it was for the evolutionist, because you already know there is a God. All that is left for you to decide is who the one true God is. Because we have already eliminated all those systems which pay homage to someone they in reality believe to be a liar, you are again left standing at the foot of the cross of Jesus Christ.

I ask you to do the only intelligent thing. Reach out for the gift of eternal life which the just but loving God of creation freely offers you when you accept Jesus as your personal Savior. While that may not be considered intellectual by any evolutionist who insists that this country's future is dependent upon his version of science (which in reality is nothing more than atheistic humanism masquerading as science), I wish to remind you that this country was not discovered by an evolutionist/humanist, but by a man who said,

It was the Lord who put into my mind...the fact that it would be possible to sail from here to the Indies... . There is no question that the inspiration was from the Holy Spirit... . It is merely the fulfillment of what Isaiah prophesied... . No one should fear to undertake any task in the name of our Savior if it is just and if the intention is purely for His Holy service...the fact that the Gospel must still be preached to so many lands in such a short time—this is what convinces me. (From the Diary of Christopher Columbus)[6]

(See Is. 40:22; Prov. 8:27; Job 26:10.)

I wish to remind you that the Virginia Company which sponsored the Jamestown expedition in 1607 stated that the first purpose for the plantation was,

To preach and baptize into [the] Christian religion, and by propagation of the Gospel, to recover out of the arms of the devil a number of...souls wrapped up into death.[7]

Let me also remind you that this country was colonized not by evolutionistic humanists, but by men who said that they undertook their voyage to plant their colony "for the Glory of God and for the advancement of the Christian faith" (from the Mayflower Compact).[8]

The first written constitution in America, the Fundamental Orders of Connecticut, recognized in 1639 that

[T]he Word of God requires that to maintain the peace and union of such people, there should be an orderly and decent Government established according to God.

The New England Confederation of May 19, 1643, recognized that the common bond between its signers was not the philosophy of secular humanism, but the desire to "advance the kingdom of our Lord Jesus Christ and to enjoy the liberties of the Gospel in purity with peace."

Allow me to point out that the Rhode Island Charter of 1683 began with these words:

> We submit our persons, lives and estates unto our Lord Jesus Christ, the King of Kings, and Lord of Lords, to all those perfect and most absolute laws of His given to us in His Holy Word.

On July 2, 1776, when the vote to declare independence was taken, Samuel Adams declared the sentiment of the day not in terms of humanistic rhetoric, but by saying,

> We have this day restored the Sovereign to whom alone men ought to be obedient. He reigns in heaven and...from the rising to the setting sun, may His kingdom come.[9]

Concerning the Revolutionary War itself, President John Quincy Adams noted in 1821 that

> [T]he highest and greatest glory of the American Revolution was this: it connected in one indissoluble bond the principles of civil government with the principles of Christianity.[10]

Let us take note that after graduating from Princeton in 1771 James Madison, the "Father of the Constitution," spent six months of postgraduate study under the private tutelage of Princeton's president, John Witherspoon. Witherspoon was one of the most prominent of the colonial ministers who took part in the Great Awakening revival which swept America between 1725 and 1760. Witherspoon spent this time instructing Madison in the principles of civil government as set forth in the Bible.[11]

In 1695 John Locke had expressed the following sentiment which in addition to the knowledge gained from Witherspoon formed the basis of Madison's philosophy of government:

> As men we have God for our King, and are under the law of reason. As Christians we have Jesus the Messiah for our King, and are under the law revealed by Him in the Gospel.[12]

In 1828 Supreme Court Justice Joseph Story acknowledged,

> ...at the time of the adoption of the Constitution and of the First Amendment to it...the general if not the universal sentiment in America was that Christianity ought to receive encouragement by the state so far as was not incompatible with the private rights of conscience and the freedom of religious worship. Any attempt to level all religions [that is, to make Christianity simply one of many religions] and to make it a matter of state policy to hold all in utter indifference, would have created universal disapprobation if not universal indignation... .[13]

This country was organized not by evolutionistic humanists, but by men who said such things as the following:

> No people can be found to acknowledge and adore the invisible Hand which conducts the affairs of men

more than the people of the United States.... We ought to be no less persuaded that the propitious smiles of Heaven can never be expected on a Nation that disregards the eternal rules of order and right Heaven itself ordained. (From the Inaugural Address of George Washington, April 30, 1789)[14]

As concerns the constitutions of the original states, *as late as 1876* these contained statements such as the following examples: Delaware's constitution recognized "the duty of all men frequently to assemble together for the public worship of the Author of the Universe." Included in its oath of office are the following words: "...I do profess faith in God the Father, and in Jesus Christ His only Son, and in the Holy Ghost, one God blessed forever more."[15] Maryland's said, "...the legislature may...lay a general and equal tax for the support of the Christian religion" and required a "declaration of belief in the Christian religion" from all of its state officers.[16] Massachusetts' constitution directed local political bodies to "make suitable provisions, at their own expense, for the institution of public worship of God... ."[17] North Carolina's stated that "no person who shall deny the being of God, or the divine authority of the Old and New Testament...shall be capable of holding office or place of trust...within this sate."[18]

In 1892, in the case of *Church of the Holy Trinity* v. *United States*, the Supreme Court acknowledged,

Our laws and our institutions must necessarily be based upon and embody the teachings of the Redeemer of mankind. It is impossible that it should be otherwise; and in this sense and to this extent our civilization and our institutions are emphatically Christian... . This is a religious people. This is historically true. From the discovery of this continent to the present hour, there is a single voice making this affirmation... . We find everywhere a clear recognition of the same truth... . These, and many other matters which might be noticed, add a volume of unofficial declarations to the mass of organic utterances that this is a Christian nation.

Finally, I wish to remind you that the phrase *separation of Church and State* is not found in the Constitution of the Untied States, rather it is found in the constitution of the *former* Soviet Union. The so-called intelligent evolutionist has once again founded his argument upon a false premise. He is either ignorant of the true facts or has once again covered them up. But that should not surprise you, for that is the history of the theory of evolution.

Eldredge tells us that "freedom to practice religion—any religion—is one of the dearest rights Americans have. Such *pluralistic tolerance can only be had in a secular society where the state has no vested interest in any single religious view.*"[19] While this statement sounds great, like the entire theory of evolution, it can only be believed if the volume of evidence which proves it false is ignored.

First of all, every single quote either from the foundational documents or from great men of America's history which you have just read, as well as those quotes which were presented in the preceding chapter, all point to but one inescapable conclusion. While it is true that no single denomination was to be given preference over any other denomination within the framework of our federal government, the teachings of Jesus Christ as found in the Bible served as the very foundation upon which that government was based. Were Mr. Eldredge to examine the 15 thousand or so documents and essays written by our founding fathers during that period in American history he would find that 34 percent of all direct quotes found in those writings were taken from a single source—the Holy Bible! As Calvin Coolidge so aptly noted, it would be difficult to support this government if in fact a majority of its citizens ceased to believe in those teachings or rejected the moral values and principles of self-restraint they entail.

Abraham Lincoln said it about as well as anybody could when he said, "...those nations only are blessed, whose God is the Lord."[20] Lincoln recognized a very basic truth which seems to have eluded many evolutionistic humanists. That truth is this country has a vested interest in the Christian religion, for without it we cannot endure as a nation. Even Thomas Jefferson, who is considered by many to be merely a deist, made this observation:

> Can the liberties of a nation be sure when we remove their only first basis, a conviction in the minds of the people that these liberties are a gift of God? That they are not to be violated but with His wrath? Indeed, I tremble for my country when I reflect that God is just and that His justice cannot sleep forever.[21]

Obviously, as a nation we cannot continue to shake our fist at God and expect His blessings in return. Perhaps this is why George Washington, when discussing the importance of morality and Christianity to our country's future, said that no man had the right to "claim the name of Patriotism who seeks to undermine those pillars."[22] (So much for "evolutionistic" patriotism.)

The greatest amount of religious freedom ever guaranteed by any government throughout history is found in the United States; but not because our system is rooted in secular humanism, which it obviously is not, or even because it is rooted merely in religious beliefs. After all, Islamic countries such as Iran, Pakistan, or even Saudi Arabia do not practice pluralistic tolerance. Governmentally sanctioned religious intolerance is also the rule and not the exception in many Buddhist and Hindu countries as well. Our religious freedom exists solely because of our uniquely Christian heritage.

The freedom to practice religion which is found in our constitution was placed there not by secular humanists, but by committed Christians. The society in which these men lived was not founded upon the situational ethics of atheistic humanism, but was anchored to the Rock of Jesus Christ. The educational system which molded the thoughts of these men was not shaped by the philosophy of evolutionistic humanism, but was based upon the principle that true knowledge begins with an understanding of the fundamental truths of the Bible, which includes Genesis chapters 1 and 2.

By no means were these men perfect. Nor were they all strongly committed Christians. They were sinners like the rest of us, but they were the first to admit that fact. As opposed to thinking that they were getting better and better, they knew that they needed to look someplace other than within themselves to find the answers to the questions which were facing them. They did exactly that. They looked to the

Bible, found the teachings of Jesus Christ, then formed a government based upon those principles.

To assume that a government based upon the premise of secular humanism is even capable of pluralistic religious tolerance is ludicrous. After all, the secular humanistic philosophy which now controls our public education system (which has itself been declared by the U.S. Supreme Court to be a religious belief[23]) has been shown to be totally intolerant of opposing opinions. Furthermore, the evolutionists are the ones who absolutely insist that their view, and their view alone, be taught exclusively in our science classrooms. Needless to say, that is not the position which you would expect academically tolerant people to take.

All you need to do is examine the record of governments which were in the immediate past or still are today totally secular in nature. There is no religious freedom in the secular societies of Albania, North Korea, Vietnam, or any other communist secular society. Under these systems many Christians face not only harassment, but imprisonment and torture. The reason for this is quite simple. By definition, secular humanism is atheistic in viewpoint, as such, it is diametrically opposed to any philosophy which calls upon or acknowledges the existence of any supernatural being.

Should you be under the presupposition that American humanists are more tolerant than their overseas counterparts, I suggest that you examine the views of such humanists as Gloria Steinem who expressed her hope that "[b]y the year 2000 we will...*raise our children to believe in human potential, not God.*"[24] Nor should we overlook the views of Kurt Vonnegut, Jr., who revealed his attitude with this statement,

"Say what you will about the sweet miracle of unquestioning faith, *I consider a capacity for it terrifying and absolutely vile.*"[25] Paul Brandwein even went so far as to emphatically state, *"Any child who believes in God is mentally ill."*[26]

When you add to these supposedly tolerant positions the fact that humanists consider belief in God a sign of weakness and that evolutionists maintain that only the strong will survive, you will arrive at only one conclusion. It is impossible for any government which maintains a totally secular position to be tolerant of anyone who believes that "in God we trust."

Chapter 9

Setting the Record Straight

At times the apostle Paul was very blunt when addressing the enemies of Jesus Christ (see Acts 23:3). Concerning the battle for our children's mind, which in reality is a battle over the truths of God's Word as opposed to the apostasy of humanistic evolution, some evolutionists have indicated that the gloves are off. They feel no compunction about referring to creationists as liars, quacks, nonintellectuals, pseudointellectuals, purveyors of a science which is in reality nothing more than double-headed, inconsistent, gobbledygook, and poor scholars. Some have even called the very God whom we worship a concocter of creation stories.[1]

As we saw earlier, Eldredge has stated that the ideas which are basic to the belief in a Creator God and those promulgated by science are mutually exclusive. He has in effect stated that the very idea of what science is absolutely and unequivocally requires that any notion of a Creator be set aside. He even went so far as to state that the idea of a supernatural Creator was "utterly beyond the purview of science."[2] However, such statements do not accurately reflect the ideas and processes which formed the very foundations of modern science. A brief examination of the facts will again set the matter straight.

In his writings, one evolutionist gives the impression that Nicolaus Steno (1631–1686), the founder of the science of stratigraphy, was an evolutionist. We are further left with the impression that any adherent to Steno's principle of super-position must of necessity deny the biblical account of the great flood.[3] The facts however show that Steno was not only a strong Christian, but that he attributed the cause of much of the geologic strata he observed to the very same flood which evolutionists deny.[4]

By no means though was Nicolaus Steno the only Bible-believing scientist. In 1864, 717 scientists, including 86 from the prestigious Fellows of the Royal Society in London, signed the "Declaration of Students of the Natural and Physical Sciences." The stated purpose of this document was to reaffirm its signers' belief in the scientific integrity of the Bible.[5] Today there are over seven hundred academically accredited scientists who belong to the Creation Research Society alone, which is only one of over a hundred different creationist societies in the world today. Every one of the men and women who belong to the CRS not only reject all forms of Darwinian evolution, but subscribe to a literal interpretation of Genesis chapters 1 and 2.[6] Furthermore, there are undoubtedly thousands of other Christian scientists who have not spoken out publicly on this issue.

What we find as we probe deeper into this subject is that instead of removing God from science, true science actually directs our attention toward God. Dr. Werner von Braun

(1912–1977), the German-American rocket scientist who helped pioneer the American space program and who became director of NASA, stated, "Manned space flight…has opened…a tiny door for viewing the awesome reaches of space. An outlook through this peephole…? shall only *confirm our belief in the certainty of its Creator.*"[7]

Earlier in this century Paul Lemoins (1878–1940), past president of the Geological Society of France, past director of the Natural History Museum of Paris, and himself a former staunch evolutionist, eventually abandoned "lord chance" after years of study. Having seen the hand of God everywhere he looked, he came to the conclusion that "the theory of evolution is impossible."[8] Stepping back still further in time, we find that Lord William Thompson Kelvin (1824–1907), the physicist/mathematician who, among other things, established the scale of absolute temperatures which bears his name and is known as the father of thermodynamics and who supervised the design and installation of the first trans-Atlantic cable was a strong Christian. Concerning the theory of evolution, he was quoted as saying that "with regard to the origin of life, *science…positively affirms creative power.*"[9]

Moving all the way back to the very beginnings of scientific inquiry, we come to Galileo Galilei and Sir Isaac Newton. These two men are universally recognized as the founders of modern science in that they were among the first to

> 1. Organize their research into ·patterns of coherent analysis
> 2. Recognize the fact that there were uniform rules which governed all natural events.

Both of these concepts meant that it was now possible to develop testing procedures which could be duplicated by other researchers in order to verify the results. In other words, these were the men who developed the scientific method which is at the very heart of modern science.

Concerning Newton's approach to inquiry, it has been said that "his intellectual method was the voice of science itself."[10] What was this method? I will allow Newton to explain that for himself:

> ...the proper method for inquiring after the properties of things is to deduce them from experiments.... [T]he theory which I propounded was evidenced to me, not by inferring 'tis thus because not otherwise...but by deriving it from experiments concluding positively and directly.[11]

As we saw earlier, evolutionists have accepted evolution not because it is observable, but because they could not accept the alternative, i.e., special creation (see Chapter 2, note 24, and Chapter 4, note 8). They have premised their entire theory upon the "tis thus because not otherwise" argument which Newton indicated was the very antithesis of science.

As opposed to setting aside the one true God of creation who formulated the very laws of nature which were under investigation, Newton acknowledged that he was dependent upon his relationship with God in order to develop the scientific method. As you may recall from earlier in this study, Eldredge equated the hypothesis of evolution with the law of gravity which Newton discovered. However, I wonder if Eldredge is aware of the fact that Newton gave all the glory for his discovery to the very Creator whom Eldredge denies?

In so doing, Newton, like Johann Kepler before him, acknowledged that all he was doing was "thinking God's thoughts after Him."[12] Newton took the position that even though he worked hard and researched diligently, it was the Holy Spirit who imparted these discoveries to him.[13]

While discussing the source of gravity itself, Newton said,

> ...the motions which the planets now have could not spring from any natural cause alone, but were *impressed by an intelligent agent*... . [G]ravity may put the planets into motion, but without divine power it could never put them into such circulating motion as they have about the sun... . *I am compelled to ascribe the frame of this system to an intelligent Agent.*[14]

Who is this "intelligent Agent" to whom Newton referred? Again, I will let Newton speak for himself?

> As to Moses, I do not think his description of the creation either philosophical or feigned... . *[T]here is a Being who made all things and has all things in His power*... . [B]y the same power by which He gave life at first to every species of animal, He is able to revive the dead, and has revived Jesus Christ our Redeemer...and has sent the Holy Ghost to comfort us...and will at length return and reign over us.[15]

Newton did not mince words concerning those in his day who, like today's evolutionistic humanists, denied God. He felt that atheism was not only senseless, but that it was actually odious to mankind.[16] By no means though was he the only scientist who shared such sentiments. There have been many since who have expressed similar views.

Jean Henri Casimir Fabre, a French naturalist who was a contemporary of Louis Pasteur and himself a recipient of the Legion of Honor for his scientific research, expressed his views as follows: "Without Him [God] I understand nothing; without Him all is darkness... . Every period has its manias. I regard atheism as a mania. It is the malady of the age. You could take my skin from me more easily than my faith in God."[17] Like most diseases, the malady of atheism has an adverse effect upon those who suffer from it. The nature of this effect was described by William Herschel (1738–1822), the noted astronomer who discovered the planet Uranus. Not only did Herschel view the universe as God's handiwork, but he observed that the "undevout astronomer must be mad."[18]

Let's pause for just a moment and examine the logic behind Herschel's statement. By stating that there is no God, supposedly intelligent atheists are maintaining the correctness of what is in reality a universal negative. To say that there is no God is the same as saying that no where in the universe is there such a thing as God. To say this you must know all about the universe. If you knew all about the universe, you would be omniscient (all-knowing). If you were omniscient, you would be God; and to deny your own existence is the height of insanity.

Sir Isaac Newton also noticed the detrimental effect which atheism has upon the mental capacity of its adherents when he said that to believe

> ...that gravity should be innate, inherent and essential to matter, so that one body may act upon another at a distance through a vacuum, without the mediation of anything else, by and through which their action and

force may be conveyed from one to another, *is to me so great an absurdity that I believe no man who has in philosophical matters a competent faculty of thinking can ever fall into it... .*[19]

It would appear that the evolutionists who insist that only evolution be taught in our schools are not only advocating a policy which Clarence Darrow maintained was bigoted, but by maintaining that gravity is innate to matter (as they are forced to do since they have denied God) they have also opened themselves up to Newton's charge that they are devoid of a competent faculty of thinking.

Think about what you have just read for a moment. Sir Isaac Newton, who has been described as "one of the greatest names in the history of human thought,"[20] said that it was the Holy Spirit who revealed to him within an 18-month period the laws of gravitation, the foundations of the science of spectrum analysis, and that branch of mathematics known as calculus. He also said that anyone who would maintain that gravity was inherent to material objects must be intellectually impaired. Yet, evolutionists of much less renown have had the unmitigated gall to say that God and science are an incompatible combination.

The atheist and evolutionist Madalyn Murray O'Hair, who filed suit to have prayer removed from our public schools, says that "Science is based on reason. Religion is based on faith. The increase of the influence of one means a decrease in the influence of the other."[22] But Louis Pasteur, the father of the sciences of bacteriology and biochemistry, said, "The more I know, the more does my faith approach that of a Breton peasant. Could I but know all, I would have the faith of a Breton 'easant woman."[23]

The evolutionistic astronomer Owen Gingerich of Harvard University says, "...I believe the heavens declare the glory of God only to people who've made a religious commitment."[24] But Johann Kepler, the father of physical astronomy, said, "Since we astronomers are priests of the highest God in regard to the book of nature, it befits us to be thoughtful, not of the glory of our minds, but rather, above all else, of the Glory of God."[25]

The evolutionist/anthropologist Richard Leakey says that the crowning achievement of his profession will be to amass data "to the point where it is simply outrageous to doubt that man is the product of an evolutionary sequence."[26] But James Simpson, the father of both gynecological medicine and anesthesiology, said that his greatest discovery was that "I have a Saviour."[27]

The humanist/evolutionist Preston Cloud stated in the *The Humanist* magazine that "fundamentalist creationism is not a science, but a form of anti-science."[28] But Joseph Lister, the father of antiseptic surgery, wrote, "I am a believer in the fundamental doctrines of Christianity."[29]

While contemplating the American public's apparent desire to take back its schools from evolutionistic humanists, Eldredge noted that "I am none the less sickened by the evidence of real creationist success in the minds of the American public... ."[30] On the other hand, Lord Kelvin actually taught his students at the University of Glasgow to actively seek the mind of God. He began each morning's lecture with a prayer which included this request, "...that all our doings may be ordered by Thy divine governance."[31]

You now have a choice. You can join ranks of evolutionists and accept their version of science which denies God, or you can accept the statements of the fathers of modern science and acknowledge along with them that it was the very same God whom the evolutionists deny who created the universe and then set into motion the laws of nature which are at the very heart of the scientific method. These great men of science were creationists in that they unhesitatingly rejected the already existent philosophy of evolution as a plausible explanation for the origin of the species.

Which is the intelligent choice? On one hand you have the evolutionists' train of thought, which even Colin Patterson acknowledged conveys nothing but "antiknowledge." On the other you have the true science of such creationists as Michael Farady, the father of electromagnetics; Matthew Maury, the father of oceanography; John Ray, the father of modern biology; Robert Boyle, the father of chemistry; Charles Babbage, the father of computer science; Blaise Pascal, the father of both hydrodynamics and mathematical probabilities, and the more than 40 other founders of various branches of modern science who also denied that the philosophy of evolution, in any of its forms, is scientific, using the true sense of the word.

To the Christian who felt that he could accept both God and evolution, I shall close this study with these thoughts. The theory of the origin of the species as presented by evolutionists is not scientific. As we have clearly seen, at various points and in various ways along its chain of development, it not only violates its own supposed rules, but it also violates at least one major principle of each of the separate fields of scientific study known as physics, biology, zoology, astronomy, geology, oceanography, and mathematics. Evolution is not scientific. It is in fact an imperfect system of beliefs which evolutionists such as Professor Shapley have turned into the false religion which reveres "lord chance." As the cornerstone teaching of secular humanism, the theory of evolution has exalted itself above God and is demanding to be worshiped. You are God's temple, but it is attempting to set itself up within you as God Himself (see 2 Thess. 2:4). I therefore remind you of the words of Paul to Timothy, as recorded in First Timothy 6:20-21, "Turn away from...opposing ideas of what is falsely called knowledge, which some have professed and in so doing have wandered from the faith."

After you have so turned, do not hesitate to refute the apostasy of this teaching (see Tit. 1:9). When the light of truth is used to reveal the inconsistencies, misleading statements, mathematical impossibilities, invalid assumptions, and circular reasoning upon which this house of cards is built, it will fall with a great crash (see Mt. 7:27).

Stop for a moment and consider the following point. On several occasions throughout this book I have referred to what has become known as the Scopes Monkey Trial. As you may well know, this case came about in 1925 in Dayton, Tennessee, when a high school teacher by the name of John T. Scopes challenged the Tennessee law which forbad the teaching of evolution in its public schools. If any of you have ever seen the Hollywood movie *Inherit the Wind*, you will no doubt remember that Mr. Scopes was portrayed as an idealistic young man whose only concern was presenting his students with the truth. According to this film, Scopes was a victim of the supposedly rabid creationistic fundamentalism which so alarms modern evolutionists. (In reality, Scopes was not even a biology teacher. He was a math teacher/coach who agreed to the scheme of several businessmen who wanted to see their small community make a name for itself by being the town which challenged Tennessee's new law.)

Present-day reference books, such as *Funk and Wagnall's New Encyclopedia*,[32] inform us that while Scopes technically lost the case (he was fined a hundred dollars), the fundamentalist cause was hurt because, while under the "humiliating" cross-examination of Clarence Darrow, William Jennings Bryan, the creationist attorney "revealed his ignorance of scientific discoveries." But what were the so-called scientific discoveries which served as the justification for the teaching of evolution in 1925? If you will recall, we have already mentioned several of them. However, allow me to quickly review them. As of 1925, the following information was being presented as scientific fact by evolutionists:

1. The recapitulation theory (ontogeny repeats phylogeny)
2. The theory of biologic uniformitarianism
3. Slow evolution of horses from the now extinct *Eohippus*
4. Slow change of all species over hundreds of millions of years
5. *Eoanthropus dawsoni* (Piltdown Man) was the first modern man
6. *Hesperopithecus haroldcooki* (Nebraska Man) was an ancestor of man

7. Neanderthal Man walked with his knees permanently bent, his arms reaching forward, and his head thrust out on a short, slanting neck

8. The fossil record did not yet show graduated development of all species because the elements had eroded the oldest layers of rock and such evidence was harder to find

9. *Archaeopteryx* was a transition between the reptiles and the birds.

As we have so clearly seen, *every one of the "scientific" facts upon which the evolutionists hung their hats in 1925 turned out to be based upon either a misinterpretation of the true facts or outright lies!*

Obviously John Scopes was a victim; however, he was a victim of the deceitfulness of evolutionistic humanism—not fundamental Christianity. John Scopes, like his present-day counterparts, was ignorant of the truth. Like most high school biology teachers today, he taught what he himself had been taught or what he had read in the latest supposedly scientific journals of his day, which were expounding upon the above-mentioned discoveries. In reality, the only thing of which William Jennings Bryan may have been ignorant was the then current batch of eloquent fabrications put forth by his generation's atheistic humanists, otherwise known as evolutionistic scientists. Under no circumstances should Bryan be criticized for being unaware of these stories. After all, evolutionists are forced to change their story with each new discovery of true science.

Many Christians are reluctant to challenge today's evolutionists because they are painfully aware of the damage caused by the clashes between Galileo Galilei and the Catholic church which took place from February 5, 1615, to June 22, 1633. Rather than take the chance that they will again be made to look foolish, many theologians simply remain silent. This is indeed unfortunate, for in each instance—concerning both the 20th-century theologians' silence and the 17th-century theologians' attacks—these theologians' attitudes are and were shaped by false science.

The prevailing "science" of Galileo's day (which had permeated the minds of many church leaders) was in reality nothing more than the philosophical thinking of ancient Greece. Rather than base their theories upon observation and experimentation, the vast majority of the 17th century scientists viewed things through the eyes of the philosopher. These men said, "'tis thus because not otherwise." As you will recall, however, Newton made it clear that such a viewpoint was definitely not scientific in nature. Just as the philosophy of Aristotle affected the view held by the religious leaders of the 1600's, so also has the philosophy of evolution warped the thinking of many of today's theologians. Similarly, just as the theologians of Galileo's day *misinterpreted* Scriptures in order to make them fit the false notion that the earth was at the center of the universe, so also have some of today's liberal theologians misinterpreted the Bible in order to make it fit the false science of evolution.

What is most regrettable though is that just as the misguided theologians of Galileo's day attacked the true science he was attempting to bring forth, so also have many of today's biblical scholars sided with modern evolutionists in an attempt to keep the truth of creation science from going forward. But this is not the end of the story. Needless to say, the truth of Galileo's position eventually prevailed over the false science which had influenced the organized church of his day. Today, the continuing discoveries of true scientists are revealing the absurdity of the philosophy of evolution. At the same time, the "laser light" of God's Word is cutting the cancer of evolutionary teaching from the true Body of Christ.

The evolutionist/humanist would tell you that there is no absolute truth. However, Jesus Christ promised to send the Holy Spirit, the Spirit of Truth, to be with us forever (see Jn. 14:17). In so doing, He guaranteed us that God's Spirit would guide us into all truth (see Jn. 16:13). Therefore, contrary to what the evolutionist tell us, truth is not only a reality, but available and recognizable to each of us through the Holy Spirit (see 1 Cor. 2:12-15). More importantly, when you expose the evolutionists' lie, you are helping other believers who have unwittingly called God a liar by accepting evolution.

Regardless of how some theologians and scientists have viewed the Bible, either in the past or today, there is no conflict between it and true science. Numerous scientific secrets were revealed in the pages of the Bible several thousand years before they were unlocked by the techniques of modern inquiry. Columbus knew that the world was round, but not because of scientific inquiry. While he had no cause to doubt the best minds of his day who also said that this was the case, he placed greater trust in the Word of God as set forth in Isaiah 40:22. Therein we are told that the Lord "sits enthroned above the *circle* of the earth... ."

According to the astronomer M. Mitchell Waldrop, evolutionists are greatly surprised by the discovery of a gigantic "hole in space" located in the northern sky. Apparently there is a 300-million-light-year size gap in the distribution of galaxies in this region.[33] This is an area in space which is so vast that a beam of light (which travels at 186 thousand miles per second) would need 300 million years to travel from one end of the "hole" to the other. While this region itself is basically void of galaxies, it should be noted that the outermost edges of this vast expanse contain a disproportionately large number of them.

The evolutionists have every reason to be shocked by a discovery of this magnitude. Such a finding goes against the rationale of their "big bang" theory. After all, matter flying out from a central point would do so uniformly. It would not deflect in such a manner as to leave vast areas void of galaxies. Christians, on the other hand, need not be surprised by such findings because God has told us in Job 26:7 that "He spreads out the northern skies over empty space... ."

The first law of thermodynamics told us that energy is constant throughout the universe—neither increasing nor decreasing. But Genesis 2:2-3 tells us *why* this is so: "...on the seventh day He rested from all His work...He rested from all the work of creating that He had done." Since Genesis 1:31 tells us that "all that He had made...was very good," it is easy to see that no more energy is needed. As to the second half of the principle, we know that energy is not being lost, because, as Hebrews 1:3 tells us, Jesus is today "sustaining all things by His powerful Word." At the same time, the second law of thermodynamics, which describes the process of degeneration within the universe, is revealed in Romans 8:21, among other verses. This verse tells us that one day in the future all "creation itself will be liberated from its *bondage to decay*... ."

Even though I have not yet mentioned them in this section of our study, you can be assured that the biological sciences are not neglected in Scripture. In 1616, William Harvey discovered the importance of the cirulatory system. But Leviticus 17:11 had referred to the paramount nature of blood some 3 thousand years earlier. As succinctly as possible, this verse says that "the life of a creature is in the blood... ." Physical well-being is related to the blood's ability to fight infection, which is in turn dependent upon the ability of our bone marrow to manufacture healthy white blood corpuscles. But this was also clearly hinted at by Solomon's admonition to fear the Lord and shun evil because "[t]his will bring health to your body and nourishment to your bones" (Prov. 3:8). Finally, while the relationship between stress and health has only recently been understood by those in the medical profession, Proverbs 14:30 (Moffatt) made the connection by telling us, "A mind at ease is life and health."

I have cited these examples of scientific-scriptural harmony not in any misguided attempt to prove that the Bible is a substitute for a science textbook. I have done so merely to illustrate the point that true science will not conflict with the Word of God. Therefore, we should not be surprised to find that some future truly scientific revelation just happens once again to attest to the infinite wisdom and knowledge of our Creator. Not only did God put the laws of nature into effect, but He wrote about them at a time when the minds of most men were devoted to worshiping the sun, the moon, and the stars. In believing that the universe is both eternal and self-sustaining, some of today's evolutionists have apparently not progressed beyond that point.

Beware of those who are "always learning but never able to acknowledge the truth" (2 Tim. 3:7). Christians have nothing to fear from open-minded truth-seeking scientists who are not traumatized by their discoveries, for along with men like Sir Winston Churchill,

> [W]e believe that the most scientific view, the most up-to-date and rationalistic conception will find its fullest satisfaction in taking the Bible story literally.... We may be sure that all these things happened just as they are set out in Holy Writ.... Let the men of science and learning expand their knowledge and probe with their researches every detail of the records which have been preserved to us from those dim ages. *All they will do is fortify the grand simplicity and essential accuracy of the recorded truths.*[34]

There is nothing wrong with study. God Himself specifically directed as to subdue the earth. But the pseudoscience which evolutionists would foist upon us is, by their own definition, incapable of determining the truth and is therefore unworthy of serious consideration. Daniel 12:4 (KJV) tells us that in the end time "many shall run to and fro, and knowledge shall be increased."

In order to carry out God's directive, we are to concern ourselves first and foremost with our understanding of the Most High God as He has revealed Himself to us and then with the true sciences. Time is too valuable an asset to waste upon the pursuit of the *origin* of the species in any place other than Genesis chapters 1 and 2.

End Notes

Chapter 1

1. Niles Eldredge, *The Monkey Business: A Scientist Looks at Creationism* (New York: Washington Square Press, 1982), pp. 82,104.

2. Associated Press, "Humans Not Smart...," Charleston, IL *Times Courier*, Vol. 206, Tuesday, April 6, (1993), p. A2.

3. William B. Provine, "The End of Ethics?" *Hard Choices*, 1980, pp. 2-3. (This magazine was a companion to the PBS series *Hard Choices*, broadcast on KCTS TV, University of Washington, 1980.) Quote taken from Francis Schaeffer, *The Christian Manifesto*, (Winchester, IL: Crossway Books, 1981), p. 57.

4. Wilbur E. Garrett, "Where Did We Come From," *National Geographic*, Vol. 174, No. 4, (October 1988), p. 434.

5. David Bender and Bruno Leone, *Science and Religion: Opposing Viewpoints* (St. Paul, MN: Green Haven Press, 1981), p. 51.

Chapter 2

1. Niles Eldredge, *The Monkey Business: A Scientist Looks at Creationism*, (New York: Washington Square Press, 1982) p. 82.

2. Ibid.

3. Ibid, p. 22.

4. Rick George, "Extinctions", *National Geographic*, Vol. 175 (October 1989), p. 676.

5. Eldredge, op. cit. p. 22.

6. D. James Kennedy, *The Collapse of Evolution*, (Ft. Lauderdale, FL, Coral Ridge Ministries, 1981), p. 6.

7. Thomas F. Heinz, *Creation vs Evolution Handbook* (Grand Rapids, MI, Baker Book Inc., 1980), pp. 22-23.

8. Kennedy, op. cit. p. 3.

9. Eldredge, op. cit. p. 46.

10. Niles Eldredge, *Time Frames: The Rethinking of Darwinian Evolution and the Theory of Punctuated Equilibria* (New York: Simon and Schuster, 1985), p. 93.

11. Eldredge, *Monkey Business*, pp. 46-47.

12. Ibid, p. 130.

13. Louis G. Leakey, "Adventures in Search of Man," *National Geographic*, (January 1963), p. 146.

14. Norman D. Newell, "Fifty Years at Paleontology", *Journal of Paleontology*, Vol. 33 (May 1959), p. 488-499.

15. Walter T. Brown, Jr., Radio Interview, *Point of View*, USA Radio Network, October 3, 1988.

16. Kennedy, op. cit. p. 2.

17. Kennedy, op. cit. p. 2.

18. *World Book Encyclopedia*, 1985 ed., Vol. 7, p. 367, Vol. 6, p. 330.

19. Heinz, op. cit. p. 26.

20. Kennedy, op. cit. p. 3.

21. George Gaylord Simpson, *The Meaning of Evolution* (New Haven: Yale University Press, 1953), p. 231.

22. Kennedy, op. cit. p. 4.

23. Ibid. p. 5.

24. Eldredge, *Time Frames*, p. 48.

25. Tom Bothell, "Agnostic Evolutionists", *Harpers*, Vol. 270 (February 1985), p. 49.

26. Douglas Dewar and L.M. Davies, *Science and the BBC: The Nineteenth Century and After* (April 1954), p. 167.

27. Eldredge, *Monkey Business*, p. 48.

28. Ibid. pp. 47-48.

29. Kennedy, op. cit. pp. 4-5.

30. Heinze, op. cit. p. 86.

31. Eldredge, *Time Frames*, p. 179.

32. John C. Witcomb and Henry M. Morris, *The Genesis Flood* (Philadelphia: Presbyterian and Reformed, 1962), p. 182.

33. David M. Raup, "Geology and Creationism," *The Bulletin of the Field Museum of Natural History*, Vol. 54 (March 1983), p. 21.

34. M. King Hulbert, "Role of Fluid Pressure in Mechanics of Overthrust Faulting" *The Bulletin of the Geological Society of America*, Vol. 70 (Feb. 1959), pp. 115-166.

35. Heinze, op. cit. p. 32.

36. Eldredge, *Monkey Business*, p. 82.

37. Harold Westphal, *The Historian and the Believer*, Vol. 2, p. 280.

38. Ruth Moore, *The Earth We Live On*, p. 170.

39. Francis A. Schaeffer, *Genesis In Time and Space* (Downers Grove, IL: Intervarsity Press, 1972), p. 138, *Early Man*, Life Nature Library (New York: The Life Books 1970), p. 19.

40. *Encyclopedia Britannica*, 11th ed. Vol. 17, p. 159, Vol. 11, p. 643 (1910); also *World Book Encyclopedia*, 1985 ed., Vol. 6, p. 16d.

41. Eldredge, *Monkey Business*, p. 996.

42. *The World We Live In* (New York: Time-Life, 1958, Editor: Lincoln Barnett, p. 42.

43. *World Book Encyclopedia*, 1985 ed., Vol. 6, p. 16d.

44. Raup, op. cit. p. 21.

45. Ibid.

46. Eldredge, *Monkey Business*, p. 111.

47. *Encyclopedia Britannica*, 11th ed., Vol. 11, p. 644.

48. *World Book Encyclopedia*, 1985 ed., Vol. 6, p. 16d.

49. Louis B. Leakey, op. cit. *National Geographic*, p. 49.

50. Witcomb and Morris, op. cit. p. 142.

51. *Los Angeles Times*, June 25, 1978, Part VI, pp. 1,6; also Bender David Leone, op. cit. p. 50. "In the Beginning Was a Bang—a Big One" Robert Jastrow.

52. Pierre-Paul Grassé, *Evolution of Living Organisms* (New York: Academic Press, 1977), p, 9; also Andrew Snelling, ed., *The Revised Quote Book* (Brisbane, Australia: Creation Science Foundation Ltd., 1990), p. 27.

53. Professor Whitten, Assembly Week Address, University of Melbourne, 1980; also Snelling, op. cit. p. 3.

54. S. Lovtrup, *Darwinism: Refutation of a Myth* (New York: Croom Helm, 1987), p. 352.

55. Heinze, op. cit. p. 40.

56. Brown, op. cit.

Chapter 3

1. Niles Eldredge, *Monkey Business: A Scientist Looks at Creationism* (New York: Washington Square Press, 1982), p. 75.

2. N. Heribert Nilsson, *Synthetische Artbildung* (Lund, Sweden: Verlag CWE Gleerup, 1954), pp. 551-552; also Dr. Andrew Snelling, *The Revised Quote Book* (Brisbane, Australia: Creation Science Foundation Ltd., 1990), p. 13.

3. Dr. Walter T. Brown, Jr., Radio Interview, *Point of View*, USA Radio Network, October 3, 1988.

4. Thomas F. Heinze, *Creation vs Evolution Handbook*, p. 63.

5. Eldredge, op. cit. p. 46.

6. D. James Kennedy, "Creationism vs Evolution—Is Creationism Scientific?" WBGL Radio, Champaign, IL, August 14, 1988.

7. Brown, op. cit.

8. Paul Brand and Philip Yancey, *Fearfully and Wonderfully Made* (Grand Rapids: Zondervan, 1980), p. 46.

9. John Tierney, "The Search for Adam and Eve," *Newsweek*, Vol. 111 No. 2 (1988), p. 47.

10. Ibid. p. 46.

11. Ibid. p. 47.

12. Ibid.

13. Ibid. p. 50.

14. William Allman, "The Origins of Modern Humans—Who We Were," *U.S. News & World Report*, Vol. 111 No. 12 (September 16, 1991), p. 58.

15. John Tierney, *Newsweek*, op. cit. p. 49.

16. "Puzzling Out Man's Ascent," *Time*, Vol. 110 No. 19 (November 7, 1977), p. 77.

17. John Tierney, *Newsweek*, op. cit. pp. 46-47.

18. Ibid. p. 47.

19. Kennedy, op. cit.

20. Eldredge, op. cit. p. 136.

21. Eldredge, *The Rethinking of Darwinian Evolution and the Theory of Punctuated Equilibria* (New York: Simon and Schuster, 1985), p. 73; also Dr. D. James Kennedy, *Collapse of Evolution*, p. 4.

Chapter 4

1. Thomas F. Heinze, *Creation vs Evolution Handbook*, (Grand Rapids, MI: Baker Book House, 1989), p. 20.

2. Encyclopedia Britannica 1972 ed., Vol. 1, p. 983.

3. Keith S. Thompson, "Ontogeny and Phylogeny Recapitulated," *American Scientist*, Vol. 76 (May/June 1988), p. 273.

4. Ibid.

5. *Acts and Facts* Vol. 17, No. 7, (El Cajun, CA: Institute For Creation Research, 1988), p. 3.

6. "The First Days of Creation", *Life*, No. 12 (August 1990), p. 40.

7. F. Clark Howell, *Early Man* Life Nature Library, (New York, Time Life Books 1970), p. 13; also Heinze, op. cit. p. 51.

8. Niles Eldredge, *Monkey Business: A Scientist Looks at Creationism* (New York: Washington Square Press, 1982), p. 128.

9. Ruth Moore, *Man Time and Fossils*, (New York, Time Life Books, 1970), p. 345.

10. Carleton S. Coon, *The Story of Man*, (New York, Alfred Knopf, 1965).

11. Eldredge, op. cit. p. 128.

12. Stephen Jay Gould, "As Essay on a Pig Roast," *Natural History*, Vol. 98 No. 1 (January 1989), p. 20-22.

13. Ibid. pp. 20, 25.

14. Coon, op. cit. p. 39.

15. Ibid. p. 36.

16. Howell, op. cit. p. 88; also Donald Johanson, "Lucy," *University of Chicago Magazine*, Vol. 73 (Spring 1981), p. 4.

17. Eldredge, op. cit. p. 126.

18. Lyall Watson, "The Water People," *Science Digest*, Vol. 90 (May 1982), p. 44.

19. William Allman, "The First Humans," *U.S. News and World Report*, Vol. 106 No. 8 (February 27, 1989), p. 56-59.

20. John Reader, "Whatever Happened to Zinjanthropus," *New Scientist*, Vol. 26 (March 1981), p. 802.

21. Tim White, as quoted by Ian Anderson, "Hominoid Collarbone Exposed as Dolphin's Rib," *New Scientist*, Vol. 28 (April 1983), p. 199.

22. Pat Railer, "Redefining Man's Past," *The Albuquerque Journal*, (April 20, 1982), p. 83; also Donald C. Johanson, "Ethiopia Yields first Family of Early Man" *National Geographic*, Vol. 150 No. 6, (December 1976), pp. 802-811.

23. Paul Raeburn, "Skeletons in the Closet: Did Lucy Really Walk?" *Albuquerque Journal*, (Sunday, June 12, 1983), p. C10.

24. D.C. Johanson, "New Partial Skeleton of Homo Habilis from Olduvai George, Tansania", *Nature*, Vol. 327 (May 1987), p. 205.

25. Associated Press, "Ancient Kenyan Lake Bed Now a Paleontologist's Paradise," *Albuqurque Journal*, (November 7, 1984), p. C12.

26. Duane Gish, "Startling Discoveries Support Creationism," *Impact*, Vol. 16 No. 9 (September 1987) p. 11.

27. *World Book Encyclopedia*, 1985 ed., Vol. 14, p. 85; also John J. Putman, "The Search for Modern Humans," *National Geographic*, Vol. 174, No. 4, (October 1988), p. 456.

28. Solly Zuckerman, *Beyond the Ivory Tower* (London: Zuckerman 1970), pp. 19, 64.

29. Eldredge, op. cit. p. 123.

30. Ibid. p. 122.

31. "Fossil Bird Shakes Evolutionary Hypothesis", *Nature*, Vol. 322 (August 1986), p. 677.

32. Eldredge, op. cit. p. 23.

33. Chester A. Arnold, *An Introduction to Paleobotany* (New York: McGraw-Hill, 1947), p. 7.

34. J.R. Norman, in P.H. Greenwood, ed., "Classification and Pedigrees: Fossils", *A History of Fishes*, 3rd ed. (London: British Museum of Natural History, 1975), p. 343.

35. Barbara J. Stahl, *Problems in Evolution* (New York: Mc-Graw-Hill, 1974), p. 195.

36. Roger Lewin, "Bones of Mammals Ancestors Fleshed Out," *Science*, Vol. 212 (June 1981), p. 1492.

37. A.J. Kelso, in "Origin and Evolution of the Primates" *Physical Anthropology* (New York: J. B. Lippincott, 1974), p. 142; also Dr. Andrew Snelling, *The Revised Quote Book* (Brisbane, Australia: Creation Science Foundation, Ltd., 1990), p. 13.

38. Sylvia Baker, *Evolution: Bone of Contention* (England: Evangelical Press, 1980), p. 14.

39. Ibid. p. 4.

40. *Back to Genesis*, Vol. 18 No. 1 (California: Institute for Creation Research, 1989), p. 6.

41. Paul S. Taylor, "Dinosaur Mania and Our Children," *Impact*, Vol. 16 No. 5 (May 1987), p. iii.

42. Eldredge, op. cit. p. 189.

43. D. James Kennedy, *The Collapse of Evolution* (Ft. Lauderdale, FL, Coral Ridge Ministries, 1981), p. 6.

44. Niles Eldredge, *Time Frames: Rethinking of Darwinian Evolution and the Theory of Punctuated Equillibria* (New York, Simon and Schuster, 1986), p. 189.

45. Ibid. p. 188.

46. Ibid. p. 189.

47. Ibid. p. 189.

48. Robert E. Ricklefs, "Paleontologists Confronting Macroevolution," *Science*, Vol. 199 (January 1978), p. 59.

49. Eldredge, *Monkey Business*, p. 23.

50. Ibid. pp. 52, 131.

51. Gould, op. cit. p. 20.

52. Ibid. p. 16.

53. M.F. Ashley Montag, *An Introduction to Physical Anthropology* (Springfield, IL: Thomas, 1960), pp. 104-203.

54. Carleton S. Coon, op. cit. p. 40.

55. *Encyclopedia Britannica*, 1965 ed., Vol. 6, p. 792.

56. Eldredge, *Monkey Business*, p. 75 (see also p. 126).

57. Howell, op. cit. pp. 30-33; also Ruth Moore, *Evolution*, Life Young Readers Library (New York: Time Life Books, 1970), pp. 108-109.

58. Howell, ibid. p. 82-83.

59. Ibid.

60. Isaac Asimov, "In the Game of Energy and Thermodynamics You Can't Even Break Even," *Smithsonian Institute Journal*, Vol. 1 No. 5 (June 1970), p. 10.

61. Michael Denton, *Evolution: A Theory in Crisis* (London: Burnett Books, 1985), p. 330.

62. Richard Dawkins, *The Blind Watchmaker* (New York: Norton, 1986), p. 5.

63. Carl Sagan, *The Dragons of Eden: Speculations on the Evolution of Human Intelligence* (New York: Random House, 1977), p. 120.

64. Jeffrey S. Wicken, "The Generation of Complexity in Evolution: A Thermodynamic and Information-theoretical Discussion" *Journal of Theoretical Biology*, Vol. 77 (April 1979), pp. 351-352.

65. Steven M. Stanley, "A Theory of Evolution Above the Species Level," *Proceedings of the National Academy of Science, USA*, Vol. 72 (February 1975), p. 646.

Chapter 5

1. Niles Eldredge, *Monkey Business: A Scientist Looks at Creationism* (New York, Washington Square Press 1982), p. 75.

2. Ibid. p. 75.

3. Dr. D. James Kennedy, *The Collapse of Evolution* (Ft. Lauderdale, FL: Coral Ridge Ministries 1981), p. 6.

4. Eldredge, op. cit. back cover.

5. Ibid. p. 98.

6. David M. Raup, "Geology and Creationism," *The Bulletin of the Field Museum of Natural History*, Vol. 54 (1983), p. 21.

7. *Encyclopedia Britannica*, 1956 ed., Vol. 10, p. 168.

8. J.E. O'Rourke, "Pragmatism Versus Materialism in Stratigraphy," *American Journal of Science*, Vol. 276 (January 1976), pp. 47, 53.

9. David C.C. Watson, *The Great Brain Robbery* (Chicago: Moody press 1976), p. 120.

10. Frederic B. Jueneman, "Secular Catastrophism," *Industrial Research and Development*, Vol. 24 (June 1982), p. 21.

11. R.G. Kazmann, "Its About Time: 4.5 Billion Years," *Geotimes*, Vol. 23 (September 1978), p. 18.

12. John C. Whitcomb, Jr., *The World That Perished* (Grand Rapids: Baker Book House, 1988); see also Whitcomb and Morris, *The Genesis Flood* (Philadelphia, Presbyterian and Reformed, 1962), p. 182.

13. Niles Eldredge, *Time Frame: The Rethinking of Darwinian Evolution and the Theory of Punctuated Equilibria* (New York: Simon and Schuster, 1985), p. 106.

14. Rick Gore, "Extinctions," *National Geographic*, Vol. 175 (June 1968), p. 664.

15. Ibid. p. 673.

16. Ibid.

17. Ibid. p. 673; see also Scott Stuckey, "Mysteries of the Dinosaurs," *Boy's Life* (June 1989), p. 20.

18. Ibid. p. 673.

19. Henry M. Morris, *The Biblical Basis for Modern Science* (Grand Rapids: Baker Book House, 1984), p. 37.

20. Isaac Asimov, "In the Game of Energy and Thermodynamics, You Can't even Break Even," *Smithsonian*, Vol. 1 No. 5 (June 1970), p. 6.

21. Ibid. p. 10.

22. Leslie Orgel, "Darwinism at the Very Beginning of Life," *New Scientist*, Vol. 94 (April 15, 1982), p. 151.

23. Fred Hoyle and Chandra Wickramasinghe, "Where Microbes Boldly Went," *New Scientist*, Vol. 91 (1981), pp. 412-415.

24. Robert Jastrow, "God and Astronomers," as reported in Bender and Leone,*Science and Religion: Opposing Viewpoints* (St. Paul, MN: Green Haven Press, 1985), p. 50.

Chapter 6

1. Thomas Goldthwaite, "Television," *Arizona Republic*, (November 23, 1983).

2. *Humanist Manifesto I and II* (New York: Promethas Books, 1973), p. 8.

3. Henry M. Morris, *The Biblical Basis for Modern Science* (Grand Rapids: Baker Book House, 1984), p. 36.

4. Niles Eldredge, *Monkey Business: A Scientist Looks at Creationism* (New York: Washington Square Press 1982), p. 24.

5. Ibid. p. 146.

6. Ibid. p. 147.

7. Ibid p. 32.

8. David C.C. Watson, *The Brain Robbery* (Chicago: Moody Press 1976), p. 98.

9. Ibid. p. 43.

10. Loren Eiseley, *The Immense Journey* (New York: Random House, 1957), p. 199.

11. Eldredge, op. cit. p. 143.

12. *Humanist Manifesto*, op. cit. p. 8.

13. Carl Sagan, "Cosmos," *University of Chicago Magazine*, Vol. 73 (Spring 1981), p. 11.

14. *Humanist Manifesto*, op. cit. p. 13.

15. Francis Schaeffer, *The Christian Manifesto,* (Westchester, IL: Crossway Books, 1981), p. 58.

16. Ibid. p. 45.

17. Ibid.; also Will and Ariel Durant, *The Lessons of History*, (New York: Simon and Schuster, 1968), p. 15.

18. Robert Flood, *The Rebirth of America*, (St. Davids, PA: The Arthur S. DeMoss Foundation 1986), pp. 21, 29.

19. D. James Kennedy, broadcast, WAND TV, September 15, 1991.

20. Adolf Hitler, *Mein Kampf* (Boston: Houghton Mifflin Co., 1943), pp. 286, 295, 325, 402, 403, 285, 289; see also *Impact*, "The Ascent of Racism" Paul Humber, Vol. 16, (February 1987), p. 1.

21. Stephen Jay Gould, "William Jennings Bryan's last Campaign," *Natural History*, Vol. 96 (November 1987), pp. 22-24.

22. Henry Fairfield Osborn, *Evolution and Religion* (New York: Scribner and Sons, 1923), p. 48.

23. E. Yaroslavsky, *Landmarks in the Life of Stalin* (Moscow: Foreign Language Publishing House, 1940), pp. 8-12, as reported in *Impact*, Vol. 16 No. 10 (1987), p. 1.

24. Eduardo del Rio, *Marx for Beginners*, (New York: Pantheon Books, 1976), glossary.

25. Conway Zirkle, *Evolution, Marxian Biology, and the Social Scene* (Philadelphia, PA: University of Pennsylvania Press, 1959), pp. 85-87.

26. Geoffrey Crowley, "How the Mind Was Designed," *Newsweek*, Vol. 113 No. 11 (1989), p. 56.

27. Stephen Jay Gould, *Ontogeny and Phylogeny* (Cambridge, MA: Harvard University Press, 1977), p. 127.

28. Henry Fairfield Osborn, "The Evolution of Human Races," *Natural History*, Vol. 89 (April 1980), p. 129.

29. Eldredge, op. cit. p. 145.

30. Ibid. p. 16.

31. Ibid. pp. 18, 78, 85.

32. Ibid.

33. Wendell R. Bird, "More on Anti-Darwinian Scientists," *Impact*, Vol. 17 No. 2 (February 1988), p. 1.

34. Eldredge, op. cit. p. 14; also DeMoss, op. cit. p. 81.

35. Charles Darwin, "Introduction," *Origin of Species* (London, John Murry, Albemarle Street, 1859), as quoted in "John Lofton's Journal," *The Washington Times*, (February 8, 1984), p. 2.

36. Watson, op. cit. p. 84.

37. Ibid. p. 85.

38. Eldredge, op. cit. p. 29.

39. Ibid. p. 104.

40. Ibid. pp. 22, 31–32.

41. Ibid. p. 22.

Chapter 7

1. Gary DeMar, *God and Government*, Vol. 1 (Atlanta, GA: American Press 1982), p. 4.

2. Niles Eldredge, *Monkey Business: A Scientist Looks at Creationism* (New York: Washington Square Press, 1982), p. 22.

3. Robert Flood, *The Rebirth of America*, (St. Davids, PA: Arthur S. DeMoss Foundation, 1986), p. 37; also Sterling Lacy, *Valley of Decision* (Texarkana, TX: Dayspring Productions, 1988), p. 8.

4. DeMar, op. cit. pp. 128-129.

5. Flood, op. cit. p. 150.

6. *CBN University Master Plan (now Regent University)* (Virginia Beach: Regent University, 1983), p. 2.

7. Ibid.

8. Ibid.

9. Henry M. Morris, *Men of Science—Men of God* (El Cajon, CA: Master Books, 1988), p. 39.

10. CBN, op. cit. p. 2.

11. *Focus Magazine*, Vol. 4 No. 1 (Winter 1981) (CBN University Publications), p. 34.

12. Fisher Ames, "The Mercury and New England" *Palladium*, Vol. XVII No. 8, (Tuesday, January 27, 1801), p. 1. See also Seth Ames (Ed.), *Works of Fisher Ames*, Vol. II (New York: Burt Franklin, 1971), pp. 405-406.

13. Kennedy, ibid.

14. James C. Hefley, *America—One Nation Under God* (Wheaton, IL: Victor Books, 1975), p. 78.

15. Vera Hall, *Christian History of the Constitution of the United States of America* (San Fransisco, CA: Foundation for American Christian Education, 1979), pp. 401-402.

16. Marshall Foster and Mary Elaine Swanson, *The American Covenant* (Santa Barbra, CA: The Mayflower Institute, 1983), p. xiv.

17. Lacy, op. cit. p. 37.

18. John Whitehead, *The Separation Illusion* (Millford, MI: Mott Media, 1977), p. 62.

19. Hefley, op. cit. p. 74.

20. Flood, op. cit. p. 122.

21. Ibid. p. 82.

22. Carl Sommer, *Schools in Crisis, Training for Success or Failure* (Houston, TX: Cahill, 1984), p. 107.

23. *World Book Encyclopedia*, 1985 ed., Vol. 10, p. 65; also Lacy, op. cit. p. 36.

24. Encyclopedia Britannica, 1956 ed., Vol. 7, p. 297.

25. D. James Kennedy, *Moral Absolutes; Yes or No?* (Ft. Lauderdale, FL: Coral Ridge Ministries, 1981), p. 2.

26. Ibid. p. 1.

27. Rolin M. Travis, "Should the Children of God Be Educated in the Temple of Baal," *Presbyterian Journal*, (February 13, 1985), p. 6.

28. John Dunphy, "A Religion for a New Age," *The Humanist*, Vol. 43, No. 1 (January/February 1983), p. 26.

29. Eldredge, op. cit., back cover.

30. Paul Blanshard, "Three Cheers for Our Secular State," *The Humanist*, Vol. 36 (March/April 1976), p. 17.

31. Travis, op. cit.

32. Eldredge, op. cit. p. 147.

33. Paul Raebutn, "Anthropologists Dispute Over Fossil Skeletons," *The Albuquerque Journal*, Vol. 102 No. 12 (June 12, 1983).

34. David Pilbeam, "Rearranging Our Family Tree," *Human Nature*, (June 1988), p. 45.

35. Elizabeth Vitton, "Leaping Lizards? Maybe Not," *3-2-1 Contact* (June 1990), p. 24.

36. *World Book Encyclopedia*, 1985 ed., Vol. 15, p. 170.

37. UPI, *Albuquerque Journal*, Vol. 102, No. 244 (Sept. 1, 1982).

38. Thomas Goldthwaite, "Television" *Arizona Republic*, (1983).

39. Donald Johanson et al, *Lucy: The Beginnings of Mankind* (New York: Simon and Schuster, 1981), p. 7.

40. "You Decide/ Should Public Schools Teach Creationism", *Scholastic Update*, Vol. 121, No. 8, (Dec. 6, 1988), p. 15.

41. Colin Patterson, keynote address at the American Museum of Natural History, New York City, November 5, 1981, as quoted in Andrew Snelling, *The Revised Quote Book* (Brisbane, Australia: Creation Science Foundation Ltd., 1990), p. 4.

42. Stephen Jay Gould, "The First Unmasking of Nature," Natural History, Vol. 102, No. 4 (April 1993), p. 19.

Chapter 8

1. Thomas F. Heinze, *Creation vs Evolution Handbook* (Grand Rapids, MI: Baker Book House, 1980), pp. 106-113.

2. G.R. Hill, *Chemical Technology*, May 1972, p. 296.

3. Saxby, J.D. et al, "Petroleum Generation: Simulation Over Six Years of Hydrocarbon Formation From Torbanite and Brown Coal in a Subsiding Basin," *Organic Geochemistry*, Vol. 9 (1986), p. 80.

4. B.R.T. Simoneit, and P.F. Lonsdale, "Hydrothermal Petroleum in Mineralized Mounds at the Seabed of Guaymas Basin," *Nature*, Vol. 295, (1982) pp. 198-202; see also *Science Frontiers*, (July/August 1991), p. 3, and *New Scientist*, Vol. 130 (1991), p. 19.

5. Lyall Watson, "The Water People," *Science Digest*, Vol. 90 (1982), pp. 67-78; also Baker, op. cit. p. 12

6. Gary DeMar, *God and Government*, Vol. 1 (Atlanta, GA: American Vision Press, 1982), p. 126.

7. Jamestown 350th Anniversary Commission, *The Founding of Jamestown and the Church* (Jamestown, VA: Jamestown Commission, 1957), p. 3.

8. Ibid. p. 126.

9. D. James Kennedy, *The Spiritual State of the Union, 1987* (Ft. Lauderdale, FL: Coral Ridge Ministries, 1987), p. 4.

10. Ibid. p. 5.

11. *World Book Encyclopedia*, 1985 ed., Vol. 13, p. 28; also *Encyclopedia Britannica*, 1910 ed., Vol. 17, p. 284.

12. Vera Hall, *Christian History of the Constitution of the United States of America*, (San Fransisco, CA: Foundation for American Christian Education, 1975), p. xiii.

13. Kennedy, op. cit. p. 6.

14. DeMar, op. cit. p. 127.

15. Ibid. p. 164.

16. Ibid.

17. Ibid.

18. Ibid. p. 165.

19. Niles Eldredge, *Monkey Business: A Scientist Looks at Creationism* (New York: Washington Square Press, 1982), p. 142.

20. Flood, *The Rebirth of America* (St. Davids, PA: Arthur S. DeMoss Foundation, 1986), p. 32.

21. John Whitehead, *The Separation Illusion* (Millford, MI: Mott Media, 1977), p. 21.

22. William Johnson, *George Washington* (Millford, MI: Mott Media, 1976), p. 112.

23. Francis Schaeffer, *The Christian Manifesto* (Westchester, IL: Crossway Books, 1981), p. 54 (citing to *Torcase v. Watkins*, 1961).

24. Kennedy, op. cit. p. 2.

25. Ibid.

26. Rolin M. Travis, "Should the Children of God Be Educated in the Temple of Baal," *Presbyterian Journal*, (February 13, 1985), p. 6.

Chapter 9

1. Niles Eldredge, *Monkey Business: A Scientist Looks at Creationism* (New York: Washington Square Press, 1982), pp. 112, 98, 22, 84, 23, 130, 10, 130, 21, 149, and 104, respectively.

2. Ibid. p. 82.

3. Ibid. pp. 93-94.

4. Henry M. Morris, *Men of Science—Men of God* (El Cajon, CA: Master Books, 1988), p. 18.

5. Ibid. p. 75.

6. Ibid. p. 94.

7. Ibid. p. 85.

8. Ibid. p. 84.

9. Ibid, p. 86.

10. H.S. Thayer, *Newton's Philosophy of Nature—Selections From His Writings*, "Forward," by John H. Randall Jr., (New York: Free Press, 1953), p. xiv.

11. Ibid. p. 7.

12. Morris, op. cit. p. 13.

13. Tim Dowley, *Eerdman's Handbook of the History of Christianity* (Grand Rapids, MI: William B. Eerdman's Publishing Co., 1977), p. 490.

14. Thayer, op. cit. pp. 47, 53.

15. Ibid. pp. 60, 65-66.

16. Ibid, p. 65.

17. Morris, op. cit. p. 63; also *World Book Encyclopedia*. 1985 ed., Vol. 7, p. 3.

18. Ibid, p. 30.

19. Thayer, op. cit. p. 54.

20. *World Book Encyclopedia*, 1985 ed., Vol. 14, p. 306.

21. Eldredge, op. cit. p. 130.

22. David Bender and Bruno Leone, *Science and Religion: Opposing Viewpoints* (St. Paul, MN: Green Haven Press, 1985), p. 32.

23. Morris, op. cit. p. 60.

24. Bender and Leone, op. cit. p. 53.

25. Morris, op. cit. p. 13.

26. Associated Press, "Ancient Kenyan Lake Bed Now a Paleontologists Paradise, " *Albuquerque Journal* (1984), p. C12.

27. Morris, op. cit. p. 52.

28. Bender and Leone, op. cit. p. 72.

29. Morris, op. cit. p. 67.

30. Eldredge, op. cit. p. 147.

31. Roy E. Peacock, *A Brief History of Eternity* (Wheaton, IL. Crossway Books, 1990), p. 149.

32. *Funk and Wagnall's New Encyclopedia.* 1973 ed., Vol. 4, p. 306.

33. M. Mitchell Waldrop, "Delving the Hole in Space," *Science*, Vol. 214, (November 29, 1981), p. 1016.

34. Winston Churchill, *Thoughts and Adventures* (Freeport, NY: Books for Libraries Press, 1972), pp. 293-294.

You may contact the author by writing:

Unlimited Glory Ministries
Frederick Kubicek
P.O. Box 476
Kansas, IL 61933